Wild Thyme
in
Ibiza

by
Stewart Andersen

First published 2007

Survival Books Limited
26 York Street, London W1U 6PZ, United Kingdom
☎+44 (0)20-7788 7644, 🖥 +44 (0)870-762 3212
✉ info@survivalbooks.net
💻 www.survivalbooks.net
To order books, please refer to page 240

British Library Cataloguing in Publication Data.
A CIP record for this book is available from the British Library.
ISBN 10: 1 905303 27 0
ISBN 13: 978 1 905303 27 4

Printed and bound in Finland by WS Bookwell.

ACKNOWLEDGEMENTS

In June 2006, I had lunch with the publisher of Survival Books, during which I mentioned that I'd written about 30,000 words of a book about my life in Ibiza, and asked him if he'd like to see what I'd done. To his credit he failed to look desperately for an exit from the restaurant and neither did he roll his eyes and mutter in despair at yet another would-be author offering him a book. The upshot is that after a surprisingly short period he agreed to publish my book – and even more surprisingly, I managed to finish it on time!

My sincere thanks to Survival Books – I trust the sales will justify their faith in me – and to Peter Read and Grania Rogers for editing and proof-reading, and Di Tolland for the layout and design. Last but not least, a big thank you to the 'cast of thousands' mentioned in the book, without whom there would be no story.

THE AUTHOR

In the late '50s, Stewart Andersen joined the Webber-Douglas Academy of Dramatic Art. At the end of the two-year course his first job was at the Edinburgh Festival, which was followed by stints in repertory in Edinburgh, Ipswich, Colchester and Cheltenham and national tours of plays such as *Charley's Aunt* and *Great Expectations*. At the same time, he appeared in TV productions such as *Z Cars*, *No Hiding Place*, *Human Jungle* and ATV's *Armchair Theatre*.

Having caught pneumonia, he was advised by his doctor to spend some time in the sun and it was his aunt who recommended, what was at that time, the little known island of Ibiza. Stewart quickly fell under its spell and he ended up spending 20 years there, accompanied by a menagerie of animals, from Labradors to an Arab horse, a pair of doves to a Siamese cat. During this time he began writing about overseas property which he continues to do to this day.

Over the years he has hosted his own radio show, written for national newspapers such as *The Independent*, *The Sunday Times*, *The Sunday Express* and the *Irish Independent*. He has also broadcast on radio and appeared on television on numerous occasions, as well as contributing to and editing several magazines such as *Homes Overseas*, *Boardroom*, *Overseas Property Professional* and the *Evening Standard* supplement, *Overseas Homes*. He is currently editor of *Overseas Property TV* magazine. He divides his time between London and Suffolk and frequently travels to France, Spain and the United States.

CONTENTS

I will always be grateful to Ibiza and the many and varied people who live there and for all that I learned during my stay on the island. Ibicencos deal with everything life throws at them with grace, courage and good humour.

❧

This book is in memory of Adelfa. A little horse who brought pleasure to many and who founded a dynasty all of her own.

❧

It is also in memory of Susan, whose gentleness touched everyone who met her.

❧

And finally, this book is for Maureen, with all my love and thanks for her patience, encouragement and for a lifetime of giggles.

INTRODUCTION

Spain in 1966 was a land caught between two eras. The old Spain was a country of kind, honest and talented people who had been held back by Fascism for decades. The new Spain materialised when *El Caudillo*, Generalissimo Francisco Franco, died in the mid-'70s. All the country's pent-up hunger for learning and knowledge exploded into life as Spain charged headlong into the last quarter of the 20th century.

For me, arriving in Ibiza in 1966 was the beginning of a love affair with Spain that has endured to this day. I love the Spanish attitude to disasters, big and small, where the only thing that gets hurt is pomposity or officialdom.

I remember once sitting at a bar in a port in my early days in Spain watching as a German-owned Mercedes, a seriously-large and expensive car, was being loaded into the hold of an inter-island ferry. The way it was done before roll-on/roll-off ferries was to lower a large and very strong net flat onto the quay. At each corner of the net was a loop and after the car was driven into the centre these were attached to a large hook lowered from a crane. In this instance, the hook was lowered, the loops were slipped over it and the crane operator began the laborious process of lifting the car and transferring it to a large opening in the deck which led to the hold.

Unfortunately, something happened inside the crane's ancient mechanism and instead of stopping in the correct place over the deck, the crane, the net and the luxurious Mercedes rotated until the car was suspended in almost exactly the opposite position from where it had come, about 70 feet above the unpleasantly grubby harbour water. To this day I don't know whether the crane driver panicked and did something untoward or the hook and loop mechanism failed, but there was an agitated scream from the crane's cab as the operator watched in horror as the net fell open and gravity took the car water-wards.

There was a whiplash effect as the crane was freed of the burden of the car, the cable emitted a loud twang and the ferry rocked back and forth like a mad thing. The car fell into the harbour with a huge splash where for a few moments it bobbed happily like an oversized duck in a bath and then, as though it had decided it might as well get on with it, the vehicle went nose down and smoothly disappeared beneath the surface.

It's odd how these things appear to happen in slow motion, but I recall seeing the crew run towards the side of the ship, some gesticulating upwards at the crane, others pointing in vain at the bubbles erupting from where the car had vanished beneath the surface, while a third group simply stood and giggled hysterically.

By now, virtually every Spaniard in sight had gathered on the edge of the quay and to a man (and woman) they were enthralled by what had happened. At first there was an eerie silence and then the level of laughter grew and grew until in the end most of the bystanders were having to hold each other upright, such was their pleasure at seeing a spectacle of this magnitude. This was Spain and the Spanish at their enjoyable best, and it is a best that I have continued to appreciate to this day.

Stewart Andersen

P.S. The title of this book comes from the wonderful aroma that follows a rainstorm, when the air in Ibiza is filled with the scent of newly dampened earth and the perfume of herbs. Above all else, I always loved the aroma of wild thyme.

1.

The Occasional Guest

It was one of those summer nights when the air felt like velvet. The heat of the day had passed but the terrace stones were still warm to the touch. My bare feet had that pleasantly gritty, dusty feeling as I stood up. Placing my glass of red wine on a nearby table I disturbed a gecko who scampered up the wall beside me, his tiny fingers gripping firmly into the crevices as he went in search of his supper, the odd mosquito and perhaps a spider or two. I looked up at the heavens over the Mediterranean, at the shawl of stars that seemed to have been flung across the dark night sky and that were too numerous to count, and gave thanks for my decision to live in Ibiza. I was 24 years old, it was 1967 and this was as near paradise as you could find. I couldn't imagine any other way of life.

Even the dust thrown up from the dirt road as Pep's cart passed by on his way home to his farm from the bar smelled incredible, like some exotic blend of expensive herbs and spices. He'd seen the candles burning on my terrace as he and his elderly horse weaved their way past and an arm waved a salutation. *"Bon a nit,"* he cried blearily, his voice echoing down the valley. Almost as though in reply, a tiny Scops owl hooted a response, its call sounding like some weird piece of miniature electronic equipment.

Further up the valley and on the far side, a neighbour's dog, Buster, decided that he ought to make his voice heard and to tell Pep that he should be home in bed and not out drinking. The echo of his barking bounced around the hills until it sounded as though a series of Busters was running back and forth. This completely freaked the dog out and made him bark even more until he suddenly stopped and silence descended over the valley like a healing blanket. I felt I could almost roll myself up in it and for a few moments I lay back in my chair, eyes closed, bathed in the feeling that every sense was wholly engaged in being alive.

I opened my eyes and looked at the dark outlines of the hills. What would tomorrow contain? A visit to the beach? Maybe. Some work? Possibly. But I was too tired to think about what was going to happen at least eight hours away and poured myself one last glass of wine. Standing up, I looked down the valley in the direction of the sea, at the strip of burnished silver moonlight reflecting off the water. As I continued to gaze at the ripples lapping on the shore, it seemed as though one of the stars had fallen into my neighbours' house. Jan and Frieda, an elderly Dutch couple, were away in Holland and for a moment I couldn't for the life of me figure out why a tiny light was moving around inside their home.

Ibiza was the kind of place back in the mid-'60s where you didn't think of locking your front door, simply because it never occurred to anyone to steal anything. If your neighbour or a friend wanted to leave a package for you, they would either place it in the shade on your doorstep or put it carefully inside the front door. According to Margarita, a widow who lived up the hill behind me, this remarkable degree of honesty was because traditionally the punishment for theft was banishment forever from the island. Whether this was true or just an apocryphal story I never managed to find out, but I well understood how powerful a threat it was.

Awake now, but still carrying my glass plus a torch, I went down the stairs to the road and headed towards their house. As I approached it, the light seemed to waver and then fall to the floor with an enormous crash. The front door was open and I could hear a strange moaning noise coming from inside. "*Que puta*," a voice said irritably and as I shone my torch inside, I saw the figure trying to rise. Two things hindered it. The first was that its feet were inextricably tangled in the legs of a chair and the second was that it had clearly taken on board far too much alcohol judging by the wave of fumes that hit me as entered.

"*Buenos noches*," I said politely shining the torch onto my face to let the figure see who it was.

On reflection, this might not have been the best thing to do under the circumstances. "*Dios mio,*" the figure cried, "*es una fantasma*, it is a ghost," and with a terrible cry, it fell backwards once more. This time, it was just too much for the chair and a loud cracking noise indicated that it would need some serious first aid from a carpenter. "*No me tocas, Señor fantasma, por favor*, don't touch me," he moaned nervously.

"*Buenos noches*," I repeated, "I am not a *fantasma*, I am a *vecino*, a neighbour of the *Señores* who own this house. Who are you, and what are doing here?"

"*Yo?*" he asked, somewhat mystified, his voice thickened by alcohol. "Who am I, *Señor*? *No estoy seguro. Ah si,si, yo soy... me llamo Francisco y estoy buscando una copa*. I'm called Francisco and I need a drink." All this time he was lying on the floor gazing owlishly up at me. Now he'd found out I wasn't a ghost, a happy smile creased his face. "*Vd. tiene una copa, Señor*, you have a drink," he continued, peering hopefully at my wineglass.

I suddenly remembered who Francisco was. I'd heard about him from one or two people who'd run across him at various times. He came from a farm some distance away and he used to roam around late at night looking for a free drink. He was completely harmless except for the fact that the light I'd seen inside the house was a candle which, thankfully, had gone out when he fell over.

I disentangled the chair from his feet and helped him up. He wavered and showed every sign of falling over again, so I put his arm around my shoulder, helped him out through the front door which I closed firmly behind me and we set off up the road towards my house. Owing to his condition, we swooped back and forth across the road like an elderly pair of Argentinian tango dancers. "*Buenos noches, Señor*," he repeated politely each time we came to a halt for a few moments, "where do we go?"

"We're going to my house where you can sit down and have a *café solo*, a black coffee and then you can go home."

"Ooh, no, no, no, no, *Señor*, I never drinking coffee. I prefer *un buen cognac*," he explained happily.

"*Bueno*, you can have your cognac but only if you drink it in a black coffee."

"Ay, *Señor*, you are very Spanish. *Un carajillo* will be most pleasant," he slurred happily. A *carajillo* was what many people had for breakfast, along with an *ensaimada*. The drink consisted of a miniature, and very strong, black coffee with a healthy shot of cognac in it and an *ensaimada* was a round and extremely sweet pastry dusted in icing sugar.

We eventually lurched up my stairs and I deposited my new companion in a chair while I went inside and put the kettle on. By the time I returned to him with his drink, he was fast asleep, his unshaven chin hanging loosely, his head resting delicately on the back of the chair and a loud series of snores erupted from his open mouth. I considered the situation for a moment. One of the things that life in Ibiza taught you was to be philosophical and accepting of unusual situations and having drunk the *carajillo* myself, I went in, found a spare blanket, covered Francisco up and went to bed myself.

The next morning, I ventured outside to see how my houseguest was getting on, but to my surprise, he'd gone. Sticking out from underneath a stone, however, was a small scrap of grubby paper and written in pencil it simply said, "*Lo siento mucho, Señor*, I am very sorry."

For a long time after that I took to leaving a small glass of cognac outside my front door if I was going out for the evening. Although I never actually saw Francisco again, I knew when he'd been around our neighbourhood by the fact that the empty glass was placed neatly inside the front door. From time to time, there'd be another grubby note simply stating, *"Gracias Señor."*

2.
Departure Time

Ibiza first entered my life when I had to spend a week in London in my aunt Marjorie's large house. She never seemed to notice that it alternated between cold and draughty or suffocating and stifling, and as I was trying to get better after being unwell for some time, it wasn't the best of places to be. However, as she was determined to take care of me, it would have been churlish to refuse and I certainly couldn't have coped on my own.

"My dear," she murmured soothingly as the thin, probing finger of a draught pierced an ill-fitting window frame, "do have a cup of hot Bovril. It would do you so much good."

"I'd rather have a hot toddy," I replied hopefully.

"Oh Lord, you're so like your grandmother," Marjorie giggled, her freckled cheeks dimpling, her small frame rocking back and forth. "She was a great believer in the benefits of alcohol and when we were young we only had to have the slightest of sniffles and out would come the whisky bottle. Of course dear, as you know, we were brought up in China when your grandfather was alive, and she couldn't get hold of good Scotch. Nevertheless, she used to make the most amazing concoctions which always had a beneficial effect."

Her smile took her back 40 years to a time when she'd been young herself. She continued, her sentences running one into another, "Do you remember that time when you found her canary lying on its back on the floor of the cage? She immediately put a drop of brandy into its beak and it revived in no time. You know, we had a wonderful time living abroad when I was a child. You need to travel more, darling. You should go to the sun for a couple of months; you'd soon feel the benefit of it. I've just come back from a remarkable place called... oh what was it... Ibi something. I know, it was called Ibiza."

"Where on earth's that?" I coughed delicately, my lungs sounding like a rickety old heating system.

"It's a Spanish island, just a short boat ride away from Barcelona," she explained. "Your uncle and I had such a wonderful time and frankly, the cost of living was so little, we could eat and drink amazingly well. The beaches, the food, the wine, the sun every day, the friendliest of people, you must go. I've decided it and I'll fix it up. Then we'll see how you feel."

When my aunts came up with a plan, heaven help anyone or anything that tried to stand in their way. Autumn changed to winter and I found myself the possessor of a passport, a flight ticket to Barcelona, a reservation in the Hotel Excelsior near the Ramblas and a parting word from my beloved aunt. "Do give my, ah, my best wishes to a young man in Maria's restaurant in the village of Santa Eulalia," she giggled. "He was so kind and he helped me out and looked after me in every way when your uncle was called back to England for three weeks. His name was Juan."

The day of departure came and on a sunny, and really quite pleasant day, I climbed aboard a Viscount turbo prop plane that eventually lumbered into the air and we headed south-east towards Spain. As we droned our way slowly across France and over Spain, I admired for the first time the view of this huge country.

Unfortunately, the take-off had been delayed so much in London that by the time we arrived at Barcelona airport, and made the transfer to the port in a rickety bus, I barely had time to buy an ancient phrasebook and travel guide in a second-hand bookshop near the bottom end of the Ramblas. Almost before I had time to get my bearings I was heading for the gangplank and the last stage of my journey.

3.

The Ferry to Ibiza

The *Ciudad de Ibiza*, its hull covered in a delicate tracery of rust and bearing on the stern the slightly bewildering sign in Spanish, 'Keep Clear Of The Propellers', nosed its way cautiously out of Barcelona's bustling harbour, as though unsure of the direction to take. Suddenly the offshore breeze seemed to give it hope that it knew where it was going and the propeller began to dig deeper as the ship gathered speed. At last I was heading for the island of Ibiza. It was December 1966, long before the modern airport was built and two-and-a-half-hour flights, two-week summer holidays, clubbing and crowded beaches.

A small flock of gulls trailed hopefully after the ferry but in the end decided that there were easier and richer pickings back in the harbour, where ships from all over the world were moored, and they disappeared into the gathering mist. A *Guardia Civil*, a member of the paramilitary police force who were famous for their oddly-shaped hats which sat sideways on their heads, stood gazing after the ship. Swathed in a cape, he stared gloomily at the ship's wake as though the ferry was guilty of something and he feared the worst. His long thin nose drooped downwards and I felt sure a drip must be balanced on its pointed end. I waved and he peered up at me in astonishment. Nobody had told me that, quite simply, you didn't wave at a *Guardia Civil*.

Gazing back at the city, at the street lights on the end of the Ramblas haloed in the evening mist, the cable car that stretched from the harbour to the top of Tibidabo and at the statue of Christopher Columbus that stood guard over the ships that came and went, I shivered and decided it was time to turn in. The December night was colder than I'd expected and I went below to my cabin.

The smell of hot oil and diesel fuel from the engine room drifted up the passageways as I entered the small cabin that was to be my home for the next 12 hours. It looked as though the porthole had been painted shut years before and the heat was stifling. Pausing briefly to admire the brass fittings, including the ancient and ineffectual fan, I heaved my bag up onto the lower bunk and began to unpack.

I was lying back reading my guidebook when there was a knock on the door. The first phrase that I had come to, "Is this the train to Madrid?" didn't seem the right opening gambit, but I couldn't ignore the fact that someone wanted to come in. Outside, I found a steward and behind him an overweight and obviously embarrassed priest. "*Señor*," asked the steward, "You have two beds in your cabin and this gentleman, *el padre*, does not have one owing very much to the oversight. Could he possibly sleep with you and not in a chair? The Capitan has said you will not be paying for this journey if you are agreeing."

As this was my first time in Spain, I hadn't the faintest idea about the correct thing to do nor could I reply in anything but English and so I just smiled and nodded politely. The priest lumbered around the steward and grasped my hands gratefully. He rattled off something in Spanish and then skidded to a verbal halt as he realised that my Spanish was non-existent. At that point, it consisted of 'please', 'thank you' and 'excuse me' and even those weren't always in the right order.

"You are very kind man, *Señor*, and I am very grateful," he continued in fractured English, as he dropped his suitcase. "I have no bed because I am late on the ship and I am priest." He looked mournful as he went on, "Many people do not like priests on ship. They believe we bring bad luck."

"It's not a problem for me," I laughed, looking at his somewhat extended girth. "But I think I had better sleep in the top bed."

My new-found friend chuckled deeply, his triple chins resting comfortably on his collar. Putting down his battered leather suitcase which was held together by what looked suspiciously like a man's leather belt, his kindly face creased in a beaming smile as he replied, "*Señor*, I think it will be good if you do as I am not climbing very well. Please, my name is Pedro and I would be very happy if we go to the bar for a drink before sleeping." I agreed that this would be an excellent idea and, given that the ship was some distance out at sea and pitching from side to side, we rolled slowly astern down corridors that led in the general direction of the bar. As we entered, the smell of black tobacco and strong black coffee assaulted my nostrils.

"Please, *Señor*, what will you drink?" asked my new friend politely.

"As we are going to spend the night together, do you think you could call me Stewart?" I asked politely. "And a brandy would be wonderful."

"*Señor...Eduardo*," he said hesitantly. "Is that how you say the name? This is not very Spanish name, no?"

"No, no," I replied, "Is *nombre* Scottish. It is Stewart, Stewart."

"Ewart," he responded, struggling manfully with the impossibility for a Spaniard of the S, t and e at the start of a word. "*No, no, Eduardo seria mejor.*" Turning to more important matters he queried, "A brandy is *un cognac, si*?"

"Yes, thank you." I nodded in the direction of the barman who was hovering nearby. "I too will have a cognac," added Padre Pedro in Spanish. What I didn't understand was that he had asked for doubles and, even worse, I had never before encountered Spanish doubles. They looked like small buckets when the barman handed us our drinks.

"Let us sit," said Padre Pedro. We found seats in a corner of the bar that were covered in a shiny artificial leather. "And now, I must tell you I am returning to Ibiza for a while because one of the Padres in Ibiza is not well. Are you coming to the island or are you staying in Mallorca?"

"I'm going on to Ibiza," I explained. "I have been unwell with double pneumonia and my doctor has told me that I must live in the sunshine and the heat for at least three months."

"What is this pneu...this pneumo... what is this sickness? And does your profession allow you to have a long vacation?"

I explained that I was an actor and having done quite a lot of television that paid well, I could afford to take the necessary time away from my 'profession'. I told him that an aunt had spent a memorable holiday in Ibiza that summer and she had told me that I should travel to the island for a period of convalescence in the sun. Trying to explain what pneumonia was, however, was to no avail. The more I tried, the more impossible it became until Padre Pedro said, "But *Señor*, you are an actor. You must demonstrate your illness."

This was like being asked to do the most impossibly difficult audition in front a director who desperately wanted you to get the part but who simply hadn't a clue what you were saying. As I gasped and wheezed, the more the priest laughed until tears were running down his cheeks and eventually we had the attention of the entire bar. Suggestions were flung back and forth in a variety of languages and dialects and it was at this point that I discovered three things about the Spanish. The first was that they adore a 'scene' and the noisier the better. The second was that they are a nation of gigglers and the third that they obtain enormous enjoyment out of discussing illnesses. Clearly some of the bar's occupant's thought I was mental and were delighted with the possibilities that this offered. Others thought that I was having a fit and urgently suggested more cognac.

"*Hombre*," cried an unshaven man wearing an elderly business suit and well-worn gym shoes with the toes cut out, "Supposing this is a catching disease? We could all be risking ourselves."

A plump, jolly housewife looked at him scornfully. "*No sea tonto*, don't be ridiculous. Such a nice young man could not be hurting anybody. He is too kind."

Finally, by holding two empty bottles against my chest in approximately the same position as my lungs, filling them from a soda syphon and gasping at the same time, I managed to get across the idea of each lung filling with water. "*Dios mio, amigo mio*, but this is a terrible illness, the *pulmonia*, and we are lucky that you are here with us tonight It was your famous English doctor, Sir Alejandro Fleming who invented the *penicilina* and saved so many lives of those who were suffering from this dreadful illness," exclaimed Pedro. "But also at this time of the year, Ibiza is *muy frio*, very cold. December is damp month and you will quickly have the *pulmonia* once more unless you are careful." My new friend added, "These clothes that you have will not be suitable for you." He indicated the T-shirt and shorts that I was wearing. "As soon as we arrive in Ibiza, we will go to a shop and purchase new clothes for you."

My earlier protector turned on the man who had suggested I might infect them all. "Now I hope you see how wrong you were. This *Señor* deserves all our sympathy, not idiots like you saying such stupid things."

Mentally, I wondered if the pesetas that I had brought with me would cover this additional expense as I'd hardly thought I would have to buy a completely new wardrobe. While I had a banker's draft, I hadn't a clue how long this would take to arrange and I began to worry about transferring some more funds. However, the cognac was beginning to warm me up and it appeared that we were going to make a night of it. Padre Pedro seemed to have not just the girth, but the capacity of a Friar Tuck in the way that he was able to absorb alcohol with increasing ease. His laugh rang round the bar and more and more passengers joined us, including a number of Ibicencos who were returning home for Christmas or, as I learned, *las fiestas Navideñas.*

Another thing I found out on that first night was that if you make a move to show friendliness towards a Spaniard and you try, however badly, to speak his language, he will treat you like a hero. Learn to speak his language fluently and adopt the customs of Spain and he will make you part of his family. During our fractured conversation which was helped somewhat by the alcohol, I asked the Padre how I could get from the Port in Ibiza town to my hotel in San Antonio.

"There will be plenty of taxis waiting and I know some of them quite well. I shall make sure you are well taken care of," he explained.

"And do the Spanish celebrate Christmas with decorated trees in each house?" I asked.

"No, no, for us the celebrations are much quieter. Every house has a *Belen,* a scene of the *Natividad* and the *niños*, the children, are given their presents on the *Dia de Los Reyes*, the Three Kings, on 6th January."

At about one in the morning, my travelling companion and I decided it was time to retire. We supported each other as we went lurching in search of our cabin. Every time we got it wrong, laughter would overtake us again and we would have to sit on a companionway and recover. The occupants of the cabins we mistakenly entered joined in the fun but eventually we found our sleeping quarters.

Despite my having some difficulties in climbing the small ladder to the upper bunk, we fell asleep, rocked by the Mediterranean, that wonderful sea that exerts such a magnetic pull on so many people who never truly feel at home anywhere else. I already felt at home among Spaniards who exhibited friendliness and charm and I just hoped I'd feel the same in Ibiza.

4.

The Hotel from Hell

At dawn the next morning, there was a tremendous banging on the cabin doors as stewards went down the corridors making sure that anyone who wanted to disembark at Mallorca was awake early enough. Unfortunately, they managed to wake everyone else apart from my travelling companion who continued to snore like a buzz saw.

Staggering down from my bunk and clutching a head that seemed to have turned into an oversized watermelon, I washed, shaved and dressed and made my way up on deck. A chill wind whipped in from the east and the sky had the look of faded denim. The tops of the waves turned into foam and with a shiver I suddenly became acutely aware of my lack of clothing. By now, I had realised that in August, when my aunt spent her holiday in Ibiza, the weather had obviously been wonderful. Now winter was upon us.

In the distance, what looked like a smudge of smoke on the horizon had gradually become an island and little by little, I could make out the shapes of hills and the mountain range that runs all the way up one side of Mallorca. I stayed on deck watching the island grow, until a shiver shook me. I decided I'd be a lot better off having some breakfast.

In the same bar where I had spent the previous evening I found several other bleary eyed travellers that I recognised. "*Buenos dias, Señor,*" one or two murmured quietly. "*Que tal?* How are you?"

"*Buenos dias,*" I ventured, the first Spanish I had managed with any confidence and certainly when I was halfway sober. I waggled my hand in that international gesture that means, "Ask me in a couple of hours and I'll let you know," in response to their question.

I found an empty table which was covered in the whitest possible cloth that smelled strongly of bleach. The barman came over with two rolls, two croissants two pats of butter and two small plastic pots of jam, one peach and one strawberry. "*Y para beber, Señor?* What will you drink?"

"Black coffee, please,"

"*Un carajillo?*" he asked. My understanding of what he was saying came to an end and I simply nodded in agreement.

He returned in a moment with a minute cup of incredibly strong-looking coffee and, clutching it gratefully, I drank half of it in one go. It was red hot and there was a strong taste of cognac. However, instead of feeling even worse, my stomach calmed, my mood lifted and my headache receded. I beckoned the waiter over and asked him what it was. He looked concerned. "Did you not want *un carajillo?*" he asked anxiously.

"Well, yes, it seems I did," I replied emphatically, "but what is it?"

He explained the ingredients. "Many Spanish people drink it for breakfast. It is what an English gentleman travelling on the ship once said to me, a starter of the heart."

By this time, I had finished my *carajillo*, ordered a second one and made inroads on my breakfast. At this point, Padre Pedro came into the bar, his normally ruddy complexion somewhat paler than the night before. "*Estimado amigo*, you have the constitution of an elephant. I could not have arisen before now, and I could not have eaten even the smallest amount of food." He called out "*Oiga*" and beckoned the waiter who came over and asked, "*Desayuno*, breakfast, Padre?"

"*Quisiero churros con chocolate y un carajillo*," he stated firmly.

Churros, that delicious pastry that is cooked in oil and then dunked in a cup of chocolate, is the last thing that anyone with a hangover should even halfway consider eating but my travelling companion seemed delighted with his breakfast and within minutes he had ordered another *carajillo*. "This is the best recipe for dealing with *una resaca*, the morning after," he explained. "You must have a lining, a foundation, to the stomach so that the alcohol from the evening before is absorbed," he smiled as he sipped delicately at his drink, his little finger extended.

At that moment, the good ship *Ciudad de Ibiza* rounded the last point and approached the port of Palma de Mallorca. The ferry would stay for four hours and then we would be on the last leg of our journey to Ibiza. The view of the cathedral in Palma was enchanting and I gazed with interest at the city that unfolded before us. As we tied up against the quay, I realised that shops were relatively close and I had time to take a taxi into town to buy some warm clothes. Explaining to the Padre where I was going, I dived down to my cabin, picked up my wallet, passport and ticket and ran down the gangplank to the shore. A line of taxis waited for passengers who were disembarking and one of them took me into the heart of the city. It was surprising that there weren't more Christmas decorations but I hadn't time to ask any questions. The taxi dropped me at the biggest store and I quickly bought trousers, shoes, sweaters and a padded coat. What they looked like, I didn't really care – the main thing was they were warm. Back outside, I hailed another taxi and we hurtled back down to the Port about thirty minutes before the gangplank was due to be raised.

On board once more, I retreated to my cabin laden with the various packages and changed into a whole new outfit. At that moment Padre Pedro entered, took one look and a wide grin spread across his face. "*Hola, amigo mio.* Well done, you have done very well. We shall have you with us for some time in the future."

"I took your advice, Padre. It really was, how do you say cold in Spanish?"

"*Hace frio*, or in Catalan, *mol de fred*," he replied.

"I think I'll wait a little longer before I begin Spanish lessons. In the meantime, can I suggest that we go up to the bar and watch the ship leave harbour?" I asked.

"And perhaps enjoy one more *carajillo*? In one night you have become very Spanish, my friend," he teased.

As the boat approached her home port she slid past the eastern side of the island and I caught my first glimpse of the tree clad hills and its strange buildings that looked like a Cubist painter had been designing toy houses. Santa Eulalia, one of Ibiza's main villages came and went in the distance. The ancient fortress-like church dominated the village and I thought I could just make out a few people walking along a tree-lined boulevard that ended at the sea. High cliffs faced out to sea, as though defying the waves to do their worst. Leaning against the rail surrounded by my luggage, I watched the crew as they began to make their preparations for docking. They chatted amicably with passengers as ropes were readied and it appeared from the gestures that many of them were either close family or certainly family friends. I felt that tingle of excitement in my stomach that I always get when I'm arriving somewhere new.

As we rounded the lighthouse, Ibiza town appeared, its old houses stacked up the hill, the Cathedral sitting firmly on top and other buildings clustered lower down. The ship headed with what seemed like reckless speed straight for the one quay that stuck out into the harbour. At the last second, she swung round as though the Captain had changed his mind and decided to head back to sea.

With an enormous rattle and clatter, the anchor was dropped, the engines put into reverse and she came to a halt. The hull was lined up neatly with the quay and gradually, the screws moved her slowly astern. As the gap closed, voices called across from the passengers to those waiting on the quayside in an amazing variety of languages. Hands waved excitedly and one or two cried openly with joy. A gentle bump against fenders, more shouted greetings from the shore to people on the ship, commands to the crew as they threw ropes ashore and the *Ciudad de Ibiza* had arrived home. The gangplank was swung round, the door that barred access to the shore opened and the foot passengers marched down. I followed them and immediately a number of taxi drivers approached me, all asking in fractured English where they could take me. Thankfully, my friend the priest appeared and cut through the chaos. "Where are you staying, *Señor* Es…Estew…do you have a hotel already?"

I showed him the address of a hotel in San Antonio that my aunt had recommended. He rattled off something to one of the taxi drivers who opened the boot of his car and stowed my baggage. With a somewhat courtly bow he opened the rear door of the elderly Seat car and ushered me inside. Padre Pedro leaned down and suggested we should meet the following day. "I wish to ensure that you are well and to introduce you to a friend of mine. Perhaps we could also lunch together?"

I agreed happily and with a crashing of gears we shot out of the harbour, through some tree-lined back streets, past what I recognised as a small bullring and onto the main road to San Antonio. "I have the same name, *Señor*, as the town where you are staying," explained my driver. "I am Antonio and I'll be very happy to act as your guide and chauffeur while you stay in Ibiza. I will, of course, give you a special price for this service." I thought his offer over for a moment or two and it seemed to make sense.

We had already travelled some kilometres and I began to realise that, although the island seemed relatively small, and having to rely on buses might not be a good idea. I suggested that we should make a deal that he would drive me around for the next two days and then we would see how things progressed.

Antonio nodded eagerly. "We are nearly at Christmas, *Señor*, *las fiestas navideñas*, and you should visit different parts of the isla de Ibiza. Of course, for us the most important day is January 6, the day of the Three Kings. This is when the children receive gifts and we celebrate with processions and parties and we visit our families. One day perhaps you will try *salsa*, an Ibicencan speciality which we make at Christmas, but this is something families make for themselves."

At this moment, we arrived at San Antonio. In those days it was a quiet fishing village and several million light years away from the crazy club scene of today. The weather had deteriorated. Out in the bay small white waves tumbled over each other like puppies playing and the chill wind made the palm trees whip back and forth. The town seemed to have hunched its shoulders against the bad weather and I was grateful for the extra clothing I had bought in Palma. We turned left in the direction of somewhere called Port d'es Torrent but after a few minutes, the taxi pulled into the driveway in front of my hotel. A modern building with purple bougainvillaea growing up the outside, it looked as though it was in need of a wash and brush up after a particularly hard season.

Antonio helped me to carry my bags inside and left, saying that he would return the following morning. "I am not so sure about this hotel for you, *Señor*. I know of a much better one in Ibiza town. Tomorrow, I think we arrange for you to stay there."

Having booked for more than just the first night, I explained to Antonio that this might prove impossible, but he pressed the side of his nose with his finger and said, "I have a cousin who will arrange matters." At that time, I didn't realise that cousins in Spain always managed to smooth one's path. Not being Spanish, I found especially useful the cousins of friends who worked in offices such as the electricity and water companies, who could always manage to make things happen when everyone else had said it was impossible.

❧

The hotel lobby was wall-to-wall marble, imparting to its guests a frigidness that didn't seem to bode well for my convalescence. Elderly British tourists wrapped in cardigans and mouse grey sweaters, with wicker shopping baskets placed on the floor beside them sat in glum silence staring at each other in mutual irritation and in some cases open dislike as they sipped coffees and what looked like minute sweet sherries.

I was handed a form that the receptionist assured me would be given to the police overnight along with my passport. So far my impression of the hotel was that I had walked into a medieval monastery twinned with a deep freeze and by the time my luggage was taken upstairs, this impression was doubly reinforced.

My room turned out to be a fairly cheerless cell. The bed consisted of a wooden frame across which was slung a sort of metal mesh. On this rested a slightly damp foam rubber mattress contained in a particularly nasty nylon cover and finally on top of this were sheets that had been washed so many times they were almost transparent. The blankets had a grittiness that made me wonder whether former occupants of the room had used them when they went to the beach.

On the wall over the bed was a picture of an incredibly depressed-looking Old Testament prophet and a single bulb on a wooden bracket supporting a fly-speckled, parchment-coloured shade. The metal light switch gave off an unpleasant tingling sensation. In the bathroom I discovered a strange half bath that meant you had to sit up on a shelf and while your nether quarters were reasonably warm, your upper half shivered and shook in the chilly air. The state of the room might not have mattered quite so much if there had been a proper bath with masses of hot water in which you could get warm or if it had been mid-summer, but I quickly realised that the lack of any form of heating meant that if I wanted to continue to get better, I'd do well to take up Antonio's offer of an alternative to this hotel.

Going back downstairs I found the bar where I ordered a double brandy and a coffee. A collection of my fellow English peered at me disapprovingly. One of them who looked even more desiccated than the rest leaned over, peered out from under a hedge of eyebrows and murmured, "You want to be careful, old boy. It's very easy to go wrong here drinking too much. It looks as though you're on the slide already." I yearned for my companions of the previous evening and their good humour. I asked him what the food was like in the hotel. "I can't really say, old boy," his voice creaking like a worn out gate, "I just open my mouth and shovel it down." His dentures made a horrendous clacking noise as he closed his mouth once more and turned and peered gloomily out at the sea.

Dinner was served in an almost deserted dining room with an assortment of waiters and waitresses leaning against the walls. As I entered, a hungry yearning look crossed their faces like a pride of lions that have spotted their prey. "*Señor*," cried one, "you come sit at my table. No, my table is better, it has wonderful view of the *bahia*, the bay," laughed another. "*Si, si*, but my table is near the kitchen and it is much warmer," argued a third. This seemed like the soundest argument of all and I was led to it in triumph by a matronly waitress.

With an exaggerated gesture, she introduced herself. "I am Josefina, *Señor*, and it is my pleasure to serving you. I am recommending the *sopa* followed by the *pollo*, the chicken for the main course and for the *postre*, I would suggest the *flan*." Not knowing what I was ordering, I agreed with Josefina that it all seemed like a good idea as long as I could have a look at the wine list as soon as possible. She produced this from under her apron like a magician pulling a rabbit from a top hat. "I am recommending the vino de Rioja, *Señor*," she said, and within minutes, a bottle of cold red wine arrived along with a small basket of tired bread. By now, though, I was hungry and thirsty and I couldn't have cared less.

The only other occupant of the dining room turned out to be a pensioner from Wigan. When she saw me arrive, she bobbed her blue rinsed head in greeting and once I was seated she wiggled her fingers seductively in my direction before getting up from her table and weaving her way in my direction. "Hello, you look lonely, when did you arrive, I think I'll keep you company, my name's Winifred, are you English?" she said without pausing for breath once. "Ooh, goody," my new companion continued, as she spotted the wine, "you won't mind if I have a small glass with you, will you, I love having fun, you see, but there's nobody young enough here to spend my time with, are you enjoying your wine, the hotel's really lovely, isn't it?" Winifred beckoned Josefina to pour for her. "I'm here for the entire winter, I have my pension paid out here, these are very small glasses, the cost of living's much cheaper and sometimes the sun shines and besides, I could never live in this kind of luxury back home, how long are you here for?"

At this moment my soup, a bowl of frigid *gazpacho*, arrived. "I should have chosen something else from the menu," I commented wryly to my dinner companion.

"Oh no, you couldn't, there isn't anything else to choose from, there's a set menu every night, I collect teddy bears and I have several with me here to keep me company, I have a young companion back in England called Simon, he's only 39, he couldn't come with me as he has to stay and look after all my bears in Wigan, I said to him it's simple Simon, at least it allows me to get into trouble."

It was at this point that I began to have serious doubts about her connection with reality. Obviously Winifred was going to be with me for all three courses, so I swallowed the soup as quickly as I could and looked pleadingly at Josefina to bring the next course as soon as possible. By now, Winifred had made serious inroads on the wine and the bread and I thought as I was obviously her host for this part of the evening, I ought to order a second bottle. My reasoning also included the thought that if I could get her to drink as much as possible, I might be able to retreat upstairs. I picked up the bottle and waved it at Josefina who gave me a nod of agreement and also indicated that she was bringing another basket of bread.

"You want to be careful, you could get a reputation around here if you drink too much, but I like a man who enjoys his wine, I'm 72 next birthday, why don't we go into town for a bit of fun after you've finished your dinner, we might be able to have a knees up somewhere and who knows what else?" said Winifred snuggling coyly up to my shoulder. The very thought of 'anything else' made my blood run cold and I decided that, indigestion or not, I wanted the safety of my room as quickly as possible.

The main course consisted of tinned peas, boiled tinned potatoes and the breast of a chicken that must have had a hard life and died of malnutrition. The entire dish was devoid of any charm but Winifred encouraged me with word and gesture. "You've got to eat dearie, you look a bit peaky and I wouldn't want you to collapse on me, would I, or maybe I would, my father called me Winifred, he always wanted me to win a Fred but instead I won a Simon, are you enjoying that?" she cackled, pointing at my plate. The thought of collapsing on her filled me with such horror that I cleared the plate as fast as possible, to the obvious delight of Josefina.

"Have you been ill, as I said, you don't look yourself, not that I know what yourself looks like, but you haven't been well, what's been the problem, dearie?", my companion asked, a winsome expression flitting across her face.

"I had pneumonia about three months ago and I'm here to try and recuperate," I replied.

"Oooooh, pneumonia, ooooh," gasped Winifred, clutching somewhere in the region of her heart. "Oooh no, that's terrible, it was the pneumonia that carried off my Nan, she wasn't that old when she departed, maybe only a few years older than you. She visits me sometimes in the middle of the night and tells me what it's like where she is now." The word departed sounded rather as though her Nan had only just caught a train and she was calling from another station.

"I'm sorry to hear that," I murmured politely.

"It's a dreadful thing, is that pneumonia, I don't know how long you'll be around, not that I mean *you're* going to depart like my Nan you understand, I just mean here in Ibiza but I know our Simon wouldn't be jealous if I were to take you in hand and look after you, do eat up dearie, turned sideways with your clothes off I wouldn't be able to see anything of you and I do like a man with a bit of flesh on his bones." This was the only hopeful sign I'd had since she sat down next to me.

In the meantime, the pudding had arrived in record time and as quickly as the food flew into me, Winifred inhaled the wine. In a kind of dead heat we finished at the same moment and Josefina swept the plate away. Winifred looked archly at me. "Are we going to call a taxi and head for the hotspots, I love to go to the bars for a drink but there's never anyone to go with me, are you feeling a bit too weak, I could always come to your room and soothe your brow if you are, Simon and I go to play bingo three times a week, what time do you come down for breakfast, if we are going out will you wait for me while I go upstairs to collect some of my teddy bears, they do so love an evening out, I won't be a moment?" and giving a girlish skip, she disappeared off in the direction of the lift.

Although Josefina and I had only met briefly over three inedible courses, we had obviously become the closest of friends. Clearly both her hearing and her command of English were superb. She caught my eye and nodded. "*Señor*, I believe you would not enjoy the bars in San Antonio with the *Señora*. I will explain to her that you decided to retire early and that I do not know your room number. May I suggest you go upstairs now?"

My gratitude, and my tip, were enormous and with a stealthy tread I tiptoed past the lift and, like a homing pigeon, shot up the stairs to my room. I locked the door firmly and carefully placed the back of an upright chair under the handle.

About half an hour later, I heard a gentle tapping on my door, the handle was tried a couple of time and a voice called out, "Are you theah, dearest, I have something that I'd like to apply to your chest, it will help you very much, Simon swears by it, he finds it very comforting." A girlish giggle was followed by further rattling of the door handle. "Come along dearie, I know you're there."

There was a sudden silence followed by the sound of footsteps and then by Winifred's voice calling out, "Good evening Captain, how are you, have you had a good dinner, I'll come and join you, shall I, on your way to bed you say, well, as I always say the night is young and so am I." There was the sound of scampering, whether from the Captain, whoever he was, in a desperate attempt to escape – or from Winifred in girlish hot pursuit of another victim, I couldn't tell.

The following morning, I avoided the pleasures of breakfast in the dining room and instead waited in my room until reception rang to tell me that my *taxista,* Antonio, had arrived. He clucked disapprovingly at the receptionist about the state of his hotel, demanded the return of my passport, gathered up my bags and swept me out to the car. "This place is for tourist, *Señor*, not for peoples like you."

I climbed into the back of the car and sank down behind the front seat in a Houdini-like manoeuvre. "Are you alright, *Señor*?" asked Antonio, his face a picture of concern.

"Could we go as soon as possible?" I asked, as he climbed into the driver's seat, shut the door and drove off. "I don't know what you believe in, Antonio, but I think there's a kind of malevolent spirit that hangs about that place. It may be the ghost of someone called Nan. Wherever you want to take me is fine, as long as it is as far away as possible from that hotel."

"I don't understand this spirit, *Señor*? Can you explain me?"

"It's when there is some very bad energy that tries to attach itself to other people," I explained. "I've had a very narrow escape from an English lady and her collection of teddy bears."

"Ah, I believe I am understanding. This is a lady called Winifred who I had in my taxi last week. This is very scaring energy, *Señor*. She asked me to have knees up with her, and I did not understand but I explained that I am married man and I could not do these knees up things. We will make sure you are some distance away from her." And then, displaying a remarkable degree of psychic ability, he continued, "I believe you will live here many years and become *muy* Ibicenco, very Ibicenco but not with this lady Winifred." And how right he was.

5.
Settling In

I soon started to shake off the after-effects of having pneumonia, thanks, I believe, to the efforts of a herbalist friend of Padre Pedro's in Ibiza town. When I met the good Father for lunch the day after I arrived in Ibiza, he insisted that I went immediately to *Señor* Juan's shop. "Come, come, I will have no *argumento*. We are going first to his *tienda* and then we are having a good lunch." He chivvied me to the door of the shop and then bustled off, promising he would be back within half an hour.

As I entered, I was assaulted by the mixed aromas pouring from jars, pots, bunches and bundles of dried herbs and strange looking plants. The miniature establishment resembled a squirrel's nest and it was no surprise when a tiny and very elderly man wearing a cardigan, grey trousers and slippers emerged from a back room through a bead curtain. His moustache whiffled and twitched and he peered short-sightedly down his pointed nose. "*Buenos dias,*" he greeted me gravely, "*en que puedo servirle?*"

For one of the first, but certainly not the last time, my mind went blank and all I could do was splutter, "*Buenos dias.*" I promptly dried and looked at him hopefully. "Are you an English person?" he enquired politely, his voice quiet and grave, rather like an Ambassador asking after the health of the Crown Prince.

"Er yes," I replied, feeling like a bumbling idiot.

"And you are having an *enfermedad*, excuse me, an illness of the chest, I believe. Could you please explain it to me?"

"I've had... ," and my mind groped desperately for the word I had learned on the boat from Barcelona. The proverbial light went on in my head and I felt a huge sense of triumph as I blurted out, "I've had double *pulmonia* – in both lungs, that is."

"Hmm," he murmured gently, "we must act quickly. *No me gusta*, I am not liking the sound you make with the *tos*, with the cough." He began moving around the shop with a quiet certainty. First he picked up two or three large sheets of paper and with a deftness born of years of practice, he curved it round his hand into a perfect cone. Then he took a pinch here and a small scoop there of herbs and added them together in the paper cone. Eventually he had three lying on the counter, the tops folded neatly inwards. Then came the instructions.

"You must make the water hot, very hot and then cooking this into the water, *como dices*, how you say, to make *una infusion*. Let it sit for eight minutes and then take out the herbs and drinking as hotly as possible sometimes with the honey." He gave me instructions for the other two cones, asked me for 50 pesetas and sent me on my way.

Clearly he had taken me under his wing and during the next few weeks *Señor* Juan mixed an enormous array of herbs, all carefully wrapped in identical twists of paper. I made up infusions, teas that tasted so appalling and smelled so bad that they had to be doing me some good, and under his direction, gradually my lungs started to appreciate the clear Mediterranean air.

Some years later, when my Spanish was reasonable, I talked to him at length about his life and where he had learned English. It turned out that during the Spanish Civil War he had been on the wrong side and afterwards he'd been placed in a camp on the mainland. Another inmate was an Englishman and gradually they began to speak each other's language. I gathered that the treatment had been awful and when he finally made it back to the islands, all he wanted was a quiet life.

Also, in the years following the Civil War, medicines were virtually non-existent and people had almost no money. Combining his love of the country with the knowledge he had of the medicinal use of herbs, *Señor* Juan began to help those who were unwell or elderly in his quiet way and he became a much loved man

And so I spent my first Christmas in Ibiza just enjoying the quiet pleasure of the island's energy. I didn't really know anyone but I was able to stroll around the town, have a beer or a coffee, explore D'Alt Villa, the old town and walk along the Avenida España in the direction of Playa d'en Bossa. There I sat on the beach for hours and as my mind and my heart were seduced by the sea I fell in love with the magic of it all.

6.

Putting Down Roots

Spring came early to Ibiza and by February of that year the fields were covered in a delicate sprinkling of wild flowers and a carpet of almond blossom that made the countryside look as though there had been a heavy fall of snow. Where it was visible, the earth was either the deepest iron red or a pale chalky white and, as the weeks went past, tiny bee orchids appeared in the furrows left over from last year's ploughing.

For a short time, a few parts of the island were carpeted with strong smelling narcissi, and frogs started croaking in the *balsas*, the brick and stone built water tanks used to irrigate the fields. The sun had obviously decided that it should make more of an effort and gradually people were starting to leave their coats at home. Thoughts of days on the beach and long summer evenings had begun to return to those who were already residents on the island

My only real problem was that I was being drawn slowly and surely into a lifestyle that was so easy going and so different from anything I had known before that I began to find it hard to imagine ever returning to London. I'd been used to a life of first nights, curtain up, having to be on time for rehearsal and learn the next script. This new way of life appealed to the incredibly indolent person I knew existed in me. It was hedonistic in the extreme; I was really feeling better and for the time being I could afford to stay on the island. The more people I met, the more convinced I became that I had come home.

I was having lunch in the port in Ibiza one sunny day with Padre Pedro, and I'd extolled the benefits of life in Ibiza for at least two courses. By this time it was 3.45pm and even he had started about thinking about leaving the restaurant. "*Hombre*," he exclaimed, throwing his hands in the air, "you don't have to convince me about how wonderful it is here. I already know. But now you should also think about putting into the earth some *raices*, some roots. Instead of paying to live in a hotel, you should spend the money on buying a house of your own."

The trouble with a suggestion like that is that once it has been said, you can't stop thinking about it. It becomes like a genie who has escaped from his bottle and by April, I was the owner of exactly what the Padre had suggested – *una casita*. It wasn't a palace, it was relatively modern, but it was mine and I could move in immediately. The money was paid, the contracts signed and I was the proud owner of a sparklingly white house. Located halfway between Ibiza and Santa Eulalia with a view down a valley towards the sea, it was surrounded by a small 'garden', a patch of bare earth that resembled a clay tennis court. Nothing but a couple of enormous cactus grew in it but I imagined that I'd soon transform it into a luxuriant haven of green. Lizards darting across it in search of shade ran across my feet as I walked and little clouds of chalky dust puffed up around my *espadrilles*.

Water came from a *cisterna*, a cavernous room-like structure that ran under the house. Peering down into it with the help of a large flashlight, I found the look of the water was decidedly unpleasant and made up my mind that as soon as mains water became available, I would have it installed. In the meantime, I decided that every drop of water would have to be boiled. I didn't have electricity for the simple reason that it hadn't arrived in the neighbourhood and in the evening, I read by candlelight.

This was preferable to the green glow cast by a hissing butane lamp. All it did was attract squadrons of mosquitoes and moths who arrived from miles around and lined up to dive bomb me if I sat outside. The occasional bat would swoop down, drawn by the lamp's eerie glow. Also, I seem to have the kind of blood group that's like caviar to mosquitoes and obviously the word goes out, "Psst, there's a really good dinner to had from that chap. There's plenty to go round – go and try it."

Initially, I didn't go to all the extravagance of buying a car. Antonio was always willing to act as chauffeur, guide and lunch companion, but eventually I decided that I had to be independent and so I bought a minute, second-hand bright blue Seat 600. The car had a soft roof that could be rolled back and latched down and this meant that items somewhat larger than the doors could be lifted up and lowered inside. The rear-mounted engine sounded like a particularly irritable lawn mower and it managed about 60mph at best on a good day and downhill.

In the absence of a fridge, I managed to get hold of a traditional icebox. Made of wood and lined with zinc, it allowed you to keep food and drinks reasonably cool. Once a week I made an excursion over the hill and down through the small village of Jesus to the ice factory in Ibiza. There, a large piece of ice would be carefully lowered onto the back seat of the car and I would race home past the weirdly smelling warehouse where *algarrobas*, carob beans, were stored, back along the dirt road to my house where, in exchange for bottles of San Miguel beer, neighbours helped me haul the ice upstairs and into its box.

It would have been churlish to refuse to put more bottles in the icebox, and so the afternoon would drift into evening and people would disappear home for half an hour, to return with supplies of bread, salad, meat, Spanish sausages such as *chorizo*, *butifarron* and *salchichas*, and fruit. Bottles of wine would appear, some frosted and chilled from resting in the icebox, others containing liquid red velvet that soothed and calmed us from the rigours of the day. That was when everything ran according to plan.

❧

One roasting-hot Friday morning, I set off in the direction of home, ice block snugly installed on the back seat. The houses of Jesus came and went and I pointed the little car up the steep hill in the direction of home. Apart from the speedometer and a petrol gauge, the only other indicators of my chariot's physical health were a number of small bulbs that were supposed to light up at the first signs of an impending crisis. At least, that was what Vicente, the ex-owner on the road to Es Cana told me when I bought the car from him.

As I approached the crest of the hill, it seemed to have an attack of hiccups rather in the manner of an elderly dinner guest who has rather too eagerly overindulged on the port and Stilton. The rear-mounted engine stopped, started, stopped, hissed, banged and popped a couple of times, and with a sound like a miniature geyser erupting, the radiator gave up the ghost. As I peered anxiously in the mirror, I saw steam shoot three feet into the air. Clearly all was not well.

Trickling slowly backwards down to a bend where the road widened slightly, I turned the ignition off, climbed out and lifted what passed for an engine cover. It was not a happy sight. I didn't understand what had happened well enough to do anything sensible and I quickly closed the cover again. Besides, other and rather more pressing matters had struck me forcibly. I had a largish quantity of ice in the car that by now would have started converting itself into several gallons of chilled water. There was no way I could lift it out by myself and the situation appeared to be hopeless. For whatever reason, my Seat 600 had run out of water in the radiator and ironically I had an over supply of it on the back seat.

At this moment, I heard the most welcome of noises. It was the sound of Manuel the bus driver happily crashing the gears of the local bus yet again. Doubtless he was skilled in many things in life but he'd never quite learned the art of synchronising the use of the clutch pedal with moving the gear lever and as the bus climbed the hill, he was forced to change down several times. Knowing that by now he would be moving at about 10mph, I ran out into the road and waved frantically for him to stop as the bus rounded the corner sounding like an asthmatic dinosaur.

With a squealing of the brakes and one last horrendous gear change, the bus stopped about four feet from my toes.

Manuel opened the window and peered happily down at me. "*Buenos dias, Señor, que tal,* how are you?" he smiled.

"I have a problem Manuel," I bleated worriedly. "My car has broken down, I have my week's supply of ice inside it and it is melting rapidly."

A smile spread across his face. Not one of the quickest souls at grasping a concept, he liked to clarify things. "Let me get this right, *Señor*. Your car doesn't work, you have much ice inside it and you have stopped the bus because you wish to ride in it? Is this correct?"

"No, well yes, I will have to ride in it but first I need your help and that of one or two of your passengers to get the ice out of the car. It is melting very quickly." By now, the occupants of the bus had gathered around the open window. Clearly a disaster was in the making and they didn't want to miss a second of it.

One, thinking slightly faster than Manuel, asked him to open the door of the bus, as the passengers would then be able to help with extracting the ice. "Ah, *si,si,* just what I was about to suggest," he remarked cheerfully. With a hiss and a clatter, the door swung open and several of the occupants joined me outside my car. Peering in, one of them remarked on how much water was already sloshing around on the floor. "*Mira, Señor,* look, if we let all the ice melt, you could hire out the car as a small swimming pool," he commented helpfully.

A giggle swept the assembled company as another turned to me and suggested, "If we lift the ice out now *Señor*, we could put it in the bus and if Manuel drives quickly, we can get it to your house before much more melts." I agreed and amid laughter and cries of "*Rapido, rapido,*" a young man pushed the driver's seat forward, climbed into the back and started to lift the ice up to where eager hands grabbed hold of it and hauled it up and over the car's roof. It was transported quickly to the bus where it was placed tenderly on a couple of sacks across one of the seats while I occupied one on the other side of the aisle. Manuel was urged to drive with all speed to my house which he did with much crashing of gears.

My usual gaggle of friends who had foregathered looked on in astonishment as an elderly bright blue bus roared down the road to my house. A cloud of dust surrounded us as Manuel flung open the doors, a gang of passengers scooped up the ice and like an eager pack of rugby forwards, they raced to the kitchen and deposited the remains in the icebox. I asked my somewhat enlarged group of friends if they would all like a beer and without exception they agreed. Eventually, with a great deal of prodding from Manuel some of them clambered back onto the bus and with much wheezing and clanking, it disappeared in the direction of Santa Eulalia. A few of the passengers remained and by late afternoon, they had been home and returned with fresh supplies. A couple of them were having such a good time that they returned with their wives. The whole thing developed into one of those parties that takes on a life of its own. Drinks there were a-plenty and nobody needed any drugs. We were all stoned on Ibiza.

A week later my car had been towed into the garage in Santa Eulalia, a new radiator had been installed and I'd received a message that I could pick it up when I was ready. I waited on the roadside for the mid-afternoon bus. Finally it appeared and I climbed aboard. I thanked Manuel for his efforts of the week before and took out my change to pay for my fare. "*Señor*, it was nothing, I was pleased to be helping," he replied. "But there is the small matter of the two fares you have not paid from last week."

"Two fares? But I was the only passenger," I protested.

"*Si Señor*. But you occupied one *butaca*, one seat, and the ice occupied another. That means that you should have paid twice and including today's fare, which means you owe me for three tickets."

7.
Stone Walled

The morning was already hot at seven o'clock and the sea merged into the sky forming one vast dome of blue. I knew that by lunchtime the heat would have built up to such an extent that it would be best to find a shady corner and have a siesta. The alternative was to spend the afternoon on a beach having frequent swims. The scent of the rosemary and thyme that grew in front of my house was overwhelming and as I had nothing special to do, it seemed an ideal day to continue my exploration of the countryside. This normally entailed driving aimlessly around until I found a dirt road I'd never seen before and following it, which was like tugging on the loose end of a ball of string of unknown length. Even though Ibiza is just 25 miles long by 15 miles wide, the back roads through the countryside are a complete cat's cradle that lead you from one coastline to another without ever touching an asphalt road.

This particular day, I headed through Santa Eulalia in the direction of San Carlos. The road was bordered with mile after mile of dry stone walls and I was reminded of the time, a few weeks before, when I'd gone for a walk along a country road towards Santa Ines. With each step the dust had puffed up around my ankles, my legs had changed from brown to pale fawn and the air was scented with herbs growing wild in the uncultivated fields. Black fruit hung from the branches of fig trees and I took one hanging over the road. I'd been told the rule was that any fruit found outside a field could be picked by a passer-by. Biting into it, the taste burst into my mouth as I crunched on the minute seeds in the centre. I'd eaten figs in England but something about picking one straight off the tree on a bitingly-hot day seemed to intensify the flavour and sweetness.

I went on over the next ridge and was so busy admiring a *finca*, a farmhouse, which looked like several white sugar cubes hunched cosily into the hillside surrounded by pine trees, that I almost tripped over an elderly man sitting with his back resting against a wall he was building. His face was deeply tanned and round his eyes was a tracery of fine lines, doubtless from a lifetime of working out of doors in the sun. He was dressed in the normal Ibicenco countryman's well-washed blue shirt, an elderly and faded pair of trousers rolled up at the ankles and a pair of dark blue *espadrilles* that could have been the twins of those I was wearing. Lying on the lid of an old tin was a half smoked roll-up cigarette that had been carefully extinguished, doubtless because he was concerned about the possibility of causing a forest fire. By his side was a hunk of bread, some raw onion, a piece of *chorizo* sausage and a large slab of country cheese, and in his ham-like hand he held a litre bottle of strong red wine.

"*Buenos dias,*" I said.

"*Bon dia,*" he replied gruffly.

"What a work of art," I continued, pointing at the wall.

He grunted a reply. Not a great conversationalist, he hummed quietly to himself as he chewed steadily. I'd always been fascinated by the techniques involved in building a dry stone wall, which looked like an especially beautiful piece of herringbone tweed. I continued to ask about his work.

"It's a hot day for doing all this – all that hammering at the stones and splitting them."

"What are you talking about?" he asked testily, "what hammering?"

"Well, surely you have to hit the stones with a hammer several times to break them and that could be pretty tiring, working in the sun?"

He gazed up at me as though I was the one who'd been in the sun too long. "You only need to hit the stones once, using a cold chisel as well as the hammer. You have to find your way into the heart of the stone, find its grain and intuitively seek the best place to make your blow. Then it is no effort." He took another swig from the bottle and an enormous bite of cheese, bread and onion. He peeled a piece of the *chorizo* by using his teeth to start it. A piece of the skin caught between his front teeth and he used a twig to pick it clear.

"Could I watch you when you start work again?" I asked.

Clearly he was someone who preferred his own company. "*Dios mio*, do you always talk so much?" he growled. "Here, take this stone and see what you can do with the tools." He took a large piece of flint in his work-worn hands, turned it over a couple of times and then handed it to me plus a hammer and a pointed piece of steel, the cold chisel.

I squatted down and examined the stone. What on earth was he talking about? What grain? What heart of the stone? What did he mean about intuition? After some time, I found what seemed a likely point to begin. I placed the point of the chisel in a hole in the flint doubtless made by a bubble of gas several million years ago, raised the hammer and dealt it a mighty blow. All that happened was that shards of stone ricocheted and flew in different directions, causing the old man to duck and, in the process, to spill some of his wine.

"*Que barbaridad*, is there no peace?" he cried indignantly. "Here, give it to me," and he snatched back the tools and the somewhat dented rock. Blowing heavily through his bushy moustache as he hefted the stone in his hand and hummed a tuneless sound, he closed his eyes for a moment and his thickened fingertips felt the rock as delicately as a surgeon deciding where to make the first incision. He seemed suddenly to come to a decision and the rock was placed carefully on the ground. Squinting, the lines around his eyes giving him the look of an elderly tortoise choosing the best leaf on the lettuce, he placed the chisel on the exact point his fingers had found and, with the lightest of light taps, he split the stone into two neat halves. I found I had been holding my breath and I let it out with a great sigh. "Now I understand," I thanked him.

"No, you don't," he answered slightly less gruffly. "It would take you months of practise even to begin to understand. Now leave me in peace to have my lunch," and with that he gulped down some more wine and tucked into a piece of bread and some more *chorizo*. As I walked quietly away, his eyes closed and he chewed methodically, his tuneless humming following me like a drowsy bumblebee.

∽

When I first arrived in Ibiza in 1966, it was only just over 25 years since the end of the civil war and much of the island was still given over to agriculture. The older sons who inherited the properties inland counted themselves lucky. A *finca*, some fields for crops, perhaps some citrus, olive and almond trees, and above all a sweet water well, and they were quite pleased with their lot. The younger ones that were left the fields and farmhouses on the coast felt they had drawn the short end of the straw.

Much was changing around the world, but in few places as fast as Ibiza. By 1970, with tourists beginning to demand easy access to the sea, more and more hotels were beginning to appear. At the same time, developments consisting of a mix of apartments and houses were under construction and the younger sons with their coastal *fincas* were beginning to be quite chipper about their inheritances.

What hadn't changed was the Ibicenco attitude to foreigners. It's hard to believe just how accepting and kind they were. As long you didn't harm anyone, it really didn't matter what you did. And it was this, perhaps more than anything else that drew a cross-section of people to the island.

A small selection of the rich, the famous (and the infamous), the poverty stricken and the homeless, all wended their way, via Barcelona, to Ibiza's shores and astonishingly they were welcomed in equal measure. The roll-call of famous residents seemed endless and included actors Denholm Elliot, Jon Pertwee, Nigel Davenport, Ursula Andress, writer Howard Sackler, singers Nina and Frederick and that much-loved gentle man, Terry-Thomas, made famous by his many film appearances during the fifties to seventies. His house, on a hill overlooking San Carlos, became a magnet for stars from all over the world.

I became aware of two other things around this time. The first was that marijuana arrived on the island in considerable quantities and the smell of 'grass' and patchouli became common in the streets behind the port in Ibiza town. One warm afternoon I was on a beach with a bunch of friends and someone produced something like a wide-necked Thermos flask.

"You thirsty, Stew?" asked Tony from London's East End. Without waiting for an answer, he poured a pale golden liquid into a glass, added some watermelon, and handed it to me. We clinked glasses and I sipped at what seemed to be a delicious blend of the sweetness provided by the fruit, a taste of something strongly alcoholic and an underlying smoky, slightly bitter taste. I felt like a wine expert as I tried to identify what the different ingredients were. Tony burst out laughing as he saw me concentrating so hard.

"Tell me what you fink's in it, Stew."

"Obviously there's something like brandy in there," I said taking another, slightly larger swig.

"Well you've got that in one. Had some Fundador to hand so I chucked that in," he agreed. "Go on, what else?"

I described the other tastes I'd found but couldn't identify.

"Not bad," his Irish girl friend, Moira, said. "Tell you what it is. We've got rather a lot of grass at the moment. We were given it by a friend and rather than have it go stale, we tried infusing some of it like you would any herb and made a tea from it. Then it seemed to need something else to give it a bit of a kick so Tony added the brandy, I brought along the water melon and we just put it all together. What do you think of it?"

By now, the combination of the drink, the sun and an earlier swim had relaxed me to the point where thinking seemed far too much effort. Keeping my eyelids open was almost impossible so I finished the dregs in my glass, rolled up a towel as a pillow and as I nodded off, I remember giggling, "I'll tell you later."

❧

When I first arrived in Ibiza, I remember seeing a group of middle-aged women going for a swim dressed in what looked like swimming costumes from the 1890s. The arms came down to their wrists and their legs were covered to the ankles. To all intents and purposes, it looked as though they were wearing woollen wetsuits that drooped unattractively as they emerged from the sea.

The other big change that coincided with the foreign invasion was people going to the beach, stripping off their clothes and sunbathing and swimming naked. Those who did it took not the slightest bit of notice of each other, but it did cause some comment among the Ibicencos that I knew. "*Señor,*" a stern middle-aged lady asked me, "how would you like your *Señora* to go around like that?"

Her elderly mother, Maria, cackled with laughter. "*Caray, hija, el señor* is a man, what do you think he'd like, eh?"

"Well," I replied trying all at once to be tactful and to hedge my bets, "I suppose if we were alone, you know, and she chose to do it discreetly…"

Maria burst into hysterical laughter again. "He would love it. And let me tell you something, *hija mia*, so would your father have done, God rest his soul. I tell you, when we were young and first married and there weren't people around, we used to go the *playa*, the beach, and go into the water like that."

Her daughter was totally scandalised. "Mama, don't ever say such a thing again. *Señor,* I have to apologise for my mother for saying such a thing. *Ay Dios mio, Dios mio,* I have to sit down, I never heard such a thing. Mama, I'm shocked." She sat down heavily and fanned herself.

Later on, as I left their house, her husband, who'd been standing outside smoking a Ducados walked with me to the car. "*Ese playa donde todo el mundo van desnudos, cual es*? The beach where they go naked, which one is it?" he nudged me in the ribs. "You never know, I might have some business that way, I might even run into you and your *Señora* there." And he laughed so much, he dropped his cigarette.

8.

Es Pou d'es Llou

Coming back to the present, I was aware that I could see San Carlos in the distance. On either side of the road, the earth in the fields changed colour from bleached white to deep red, depending on whether I was driving through an area where chalk or iron predominated in the soil. On the right-hand side of the road was the place where you could buy the best *harina integral*, wholemeal flour, on the island. I'd found making my own bread deeply satisfying, despite the fact that butane gas cookers are notoriously unreliable when it comes to temperatures.

From time to time as I drove on, I passed dry riverbeds which, during winter storms, would turn into raging, foaming *torrentes* for a brief spell, carrying branches, rubbish, tin cans and stones of varying sizes down the hillside. Within hours they would have been swept clear and, as the rain stopped as though switched off at a tap, the *torrentes* reverted to bone-dry gullies that revealed the land's rocky ribs and vertebrae through the earth.

Entering San Carlos village, I parked in the shade of the church and went in to get a cold beer at Anita's Bar. Ruled by Anita with a rod of iron, nevertheless it was also the headquarters in the mid-'60s for a disparate group of hippies, craftsmen and early drop-outs from the Vietnam War. The odd tourist would park outside the church and tentatively approach the *terraza*. A motley collection of heads would look up and the tourist might well steal silently away. "*Buenos dias*," I said in general greeting as I entered the small, heavily shaded patio and a lazy chorus of "*Buenos dias*," "*Bon dia*," "Hi, man," "*Morgen, wie getes?*" came back from under the canopy of purple bougainvillaea.

In the bar, I asked for a bottle of San Miguel beer from the small gas refrigerator. I picked up a *Diario de Ibiza*, the local newspaper that was still 85 per cent unintelligible to me but trying to read it was one of the best ways of learning the language. I went back outside to find a chair, where I discovered that the only seat was next to an American, Katherine, who I'd met a couple of times with friends. Wearing jeans, a T-shirt and an embroidered waistcoat inset with small pieces of mirror, she was slim, attractive and very much rich US East Coast. She'd arrived on Ibiza with her Spanish partner Manolo and when he decided to move on to Goa, she chose to remain where she was. Her throaty voice greeted me. "Hi, Stew, how's it going?" she asked as she stubbed out her Fortuna cigarette. Sitting down at her table and taking a swig of the beer I explained that I was having an aimless day exploring the island. Katharine told me she was living in a *finca* near San José. "I don't often come as far over as San Carlos but I've got some friends who live near here and they asked me over for dinner yesterday, so I stayed the night."

We had another couple of beers. "I'm trying to find a beach someone mentioned – want to join me?" I asked. "I was told that if you head for Es Figueral and take a turning to the right, you eventually come to a bay called Es Pou d'es Llou. There's supposed to be a *pension* there that sells cold beer and lunch and there's great swimming in the bay."

"Sounds wonderful," she grinned, "I'd love to find out more about the island. Manolo told me that one of the bays around here was where the island was invaded during the Civil War – maybe it's your Es Pou d'es Llou."

We finished our drinks and clambered into my Seat 600 that by now was sitting in full sun. The steering wheel was almost too hot to touch for a few minutes and any exposed bits of skin instantly stuck to the seats. However, once we were back on the road the air quickly cooled us. Fifteen minutes later the road wound its way downhill to the bay of Es Figueral, but there'd been no sign of a turning off to the right. We turned round and started to drive back slowly in the direction of San Carlos. Then

I realised we'd passed a small dirt road and we retraced our steps until we found it.

About ten minutes and one wrong turning later, we arrived at a small, square building with a lopsided sign hanging from a pine tree that had once read *Es Pou d'es Llou.* We decided to take a look at the beach and found that it was covered in pebbles and seaweed and sloped steeply down to the sea. The road wound around the back of the bay and disappeared among some low scrubby pines and bushes. Parking, we walked across a wide expanse of flat rock covered in small stones and within a couple of minutes there was the sea. It was an easy climb down and it was too inviting not to strip off and dive in. There was an almost completely enclosed rock pool with weed attached to the bottom that swayed gently in the movement caused by the waves coming through a gap in the rocks, and around part of the outer wall of the pool ran a wide ledge. Nature had obviously anticipated that humans would want to swim here and quickly I went back to the car to pick up a collection of flippers, snorkels and facemasks that lived in the boot.

After the heat of the day, the water was like the smoothest of velvet on the skin. As we swam out towards some rocks in the middle of the bay, I looked down and saw that the seabed sloped away gradually. Then there was a shelf and suddenly the bottom dropped quite sharply. As though suspended in space about 30 feet down was a large shoal of minute brilliant blue fish that glittered and flashed as they turned and twisted. I dived down among them and the shoal exploded around me like a shower of electric blue sparks.

In shallower water, I'd spotted a smallish octopus. Normally the shyest of creatures that hide under shelves of rock or in deep hollows filled with rubble, this one had obviously enjoyed a meal of abalone, and their shells were lying nearby, partly on top of the octopus and some in small heaps around him. The sun shining through the water reflected off the mother-of-pearl interiors of the shells; it was like looking at a small searchlight sparkling and twinkling back at the surface.

I swam back to where I could hover over him and dived slowly down, fully expecting the little creature to disappear in a stream of bubbles. Instead, he crouched down under his brilliant roof. I held on to a large rock, put a finger down in his direction and gently touched a tentacle and again he failed to take off as most of his brethren would have done. Swimming back up to the surface, I called Katherine to come and look. Once again I took several deep breaths, went back down and touched his tentacle. This unfurled like some strange plant and he grasped my finger, his suckers tightening gently.

Sadly, I could no longer stay down there with him and I shot back to the surface once again. This time the sudden movement was too much and emerging from his hole, he disappeared across the seabed like a miniature space ship taking off, ink streaming behind him.

We swam back to near the rocks where the water was warmer and I began to explore the almost enclosed pool I'd seen from above; floating in through an opening in the rocks, I found myself in a tiny secret world. The inner walls had underwater horizontal shelves and it was on one of these that I noticed something that was a bright olive green. It gleamed in the dappled sunlight that twisted and twirled as it shone down through the water.

I swam over and picked up an inch long cowrie shell that once out of the water shone like a valuable gem. I'd swum in a number of bays around the coast of Ibiza and found many different shells but not once had I seen anything like the little object lying in the palm of my hand. I was worried that there might be a tiny crab lurking inside but holding it upside down out of the water, I found nobody at home. Finding it was like being given the most wonderful gift and I swam over to where Katherine was floating motionless on the surface like a pink starfish. Kicking her flippers, she swam lazily towards me. "Dear Lord," she said,

57

taking the snorkel and facemask off, "this is the most enchanted bay in the world. What's that in your hand?"

I showed her the shell and she let out a gasp of surprise. "Oh, it's so perfect," she murmured, taking the cowrie and turning it over. "I never knew you could find these in Ibiza. I've seen bigger ones in shops back home but I always thought they'd been polished artificially. It's *so* beautiful. Let's see if there are any more."

Spitting into her facemask, she washed it out and pulled it back on. Launching herself off once more, she then turned and swam slowly along the ridge where I'd found the first one. We both searched for another half an hour, and we found just one more, smaller, much darker and equally without anyone inside. In fact, over the years that I visited Es Pou d'es Llou, I only ever found an occupant in one of the cowries. One Sunday morning, as I picked it up, a tiny crab peered out at me with a look of absolute horror at being disturbed and disappeared swiftly back inside. On that occasion, I placed the shell carefully back on the ledge and swam silently away, feeling guilty at having disturbed the little crab's Sunday lie-in.

Eventually, Katherine announced that she was hungry and, more to the point, wanted a drink and so we went back to the flat rocks where we'd left our things, climbed out and headed back to the car. We parked at the *pension* we'd passed earlier, went in and found two enormous bonuses. The first was that they had ice-cold beer, and we drank two of these at high speed as we sat under the cane roof of the patio. The second was that they had *paella* on the menu for lunch and this turned out to be nothing whatever like the dish that was served to tourists. It had a delicious flavour of saffron, the rice had retained its texture and it was laden with shellfish, pieces of chicken, pork and vegetables. To start we had a small bowl of homemade *ail-y-olli* into which Pepita the waitress insisted we should dip *pan payes*, or country bread.

The taste of garlic erupted in our mouths and encouraged us to order a second bowl and two more beers while we waited for our main course. *Ail-y-olli* guarantees your social unacceptability for at least 24 hours afterwards but it's so worthwhile. And of course, it doesn't really matter as long as you've both eaten it. We had that delicious feeling that only seawater drying on the skin can give you and the heaviness you get after a long swim on a hot day. It's a tingling, tight, clean sensation, which, combined with sitting in the cool with a feast in front of you, a couple of cold beers and the air scented with herbs and pine trees, made life look pretty good. We sat and peered through the trees at the bay as the long afternoon drifted slowly away and decided that there was no point in ever leaving Ibiza because there was nowhere else to live.

9.
Fire in the Hills

As July blended into the dog days of August the unbelievable, for me, happened. There had been so many sunny days that when you opened the shutters in the morning and saw yet another blue sky, you found yourself longing for a grey, rainy day.

As a result of this continual fine weather, two things became apparent. There was a constant need to keep cool and this meant that the attention of most of the island's residents had become focussed on getting to the beach as often as possible, while the lucky ones with electricity became hugely popular as friends descended on them to share their fans. On the other hand, the oven-like heat meant that there was the constant threat of forest fire. You could hardly miss the enormous posters put up by the Spanish government, with messages such as '*Quien quema el monte*? Who set fire to the hillside?' and another which pointed out that it takes 30 years for a pine tree to reach maturity and 30 seconds to burn it down.

Ibiza's small rounded hills were covered with a number of different types of pine, and, according to a rumour, the Madrid government had once sent a surveyor to estimate the density and numbers of the trees. It was said that he measured off an average sized hill and set to work. However, such was the density of the forest that he eventually gave up, regarding the task as too great and returned to his Ministry in Madrid.

Each summer, the heat brought the terrible threat of fire to the island. What the sun gave us in the way of suntans and long lazy days on the beach had to be paid for with the ever-present risk of fire. Careless tourists who didn't understand these perils were the cause of terrible blazes; smokers who threw the remains of their cigarettes out of their car windows could easily leave a trail of devastation in their path. I'd been involved in helping to fight a fire quite near my house the month before. In my case, the *Guardia Civil* quickly discovered that some tourists who'd been camping in the woods had made supper using a small gas stove that they'd placed on the ground. They finally went to bed, leaving the stove alight. Just how it came to tip over, we'll never know but they were responsible for setting fire to half a hillside before it was brought under control.

There was the additional hazard that pine trees contain highly inflammable resin. It had the tendency to make the trees explode when they were exposed to great heat. This in turn would fling burning embers from tree to tree, spreading a fire faster than a person could run. There's no more terrible sight than that first tendril of smoke curling up from a hillside.

We would all hope that someone was burning rubbish, but as the smoke grew denser it would become obvious that once again, part of our environment was in danger. At that time there was an unwritten rule that when there was a forest fire, every able-bodied person had to do their best to help, whether trying to contain the fire until professionals arrived or carrying water to those tackling the blaze. The professionals included some of those brave pilots who fly the planes that skim along the surface of the sea or a lake, suck an enormous quantity of water into the hold, fly low over the fire and bomb it, hopefully extinguishing it as soon as possible. It's an incredibly dangerous occupation, because the pilot has to cope not just with getting the water in the right place, but also with the up-draught from the fire and the sudden change in weight as the water drops from the aircraft.

One evening, Katherine and I were returning home from dinner with a couple who lived towards Playa d'en Bossa. We were driving along the back road from Jesus when we spotted a golden glow in the sky. It wasn't particularly late and I remarked, "Looks as though Alicia and Tom are having a pretty big barbecue. Let's see." And so we turned off to the left onto a much smaller and heavily rutted *camino*. Our friends lived about half a kilometre off the main road and we hadn't travelled more than a couple of hundred metres when we became aware of the unmistakable smell of burning pine. Turning the corner, we nearly ran into Alicia driving frantically down the road. When she saw our car, she skidded to a halt. "Quick, the hillside above the house is on fire. We have to get help, the *bomberos,* the fire brigade and we have to tell the *Guardia Civil*."

Katherine agreed to drive as fast as possible to Santa Eulalia for help while I returned to the house with Alicia to see what the three of us could do. At that time, there were precious few phones on the island, let alone mobiles and walkie talkies, and the only thing to do was to trust to luck and drive as fast as you could.

Being an organised man and living as close as he did to woods, Tom had kept a stack of cut branches suitable for beating at the flames ready for just such an emergency. They were stored in his *almacen*, a barn, and when we arrived, he was working hard at a hand pump, frantically filling as many containers as possible from his well. Alicia took over the pumping while Tom and I grabbed branches and a small axe each and headed up the hillside to see just how bad it was. The fire was being driven by a light breeze and it seemed to be heading at an angle that might just, with a bit of luck, take it away from his house. A small front of the fire was burning all the dry tinder, grass and herbs and this was something we could begin to tackle.

But you couldn't leave anything to chance, and no sooner had we started on the bottom edge of the fire, than the flames seemed to rear up further along the hill. Any of nature's extreme conditions can be scary, whether it's a hurricane, a snow avalanche or flooding, but there's something especially malevolent about a fire that's taken hold in a pine forest, where you can be safe one minute and encircled by flames the next.

The branches Tom had stored came from a bush that was known to be pretty resistant to the fire, but we quickly realised that unless help arrived soon, our attempts would be too little and much too late. The fire was jumping from tree-top to tree-top and as fast as we managed to stop it in one corner, it erupted elsewhere.

There's the ever-present danger of being encircled by the flames and we were just beginning to despair when we spotted what looked like a cavalcade of cars coming up the valley. In minutes neighbours began to join us on the hillside, each one equipped with branches, saws and axes. I called across to Jaume, the owner of a bar on the road to Santa Eulalia, "How did you get here so soon?"

He shouted back above the crackling and roar of the flames, "Several of us were enjoying a quiet drink when your *amiga, la Señorita* Katerina came in like the *diablo*, the devil was after her, and told us what had happened and so we came immediately. She has gone to Santa Eulalia to get more help. Here," he went on, "I brought you both a present."

He came over to where Tom and I were taking a breather and from his pockets, he produced two bottle of San Miguel beer. "Oh no, we haven't got an *abretapas*, a bottle opener," I groaned.

"*Ningun problema*, that's easy," laughed Jaume and like any good Spanish bar owner, he placed the lip of the cap on each bottle in turn on the edge of a rock and smacked his hand down firmly on the top. Beer frothed up as the cap flew off and we each grabbed urgently at our gifts. "*Salud,*" we toasted him gratefully. "*Salud,*" he replied as he went back to fighting the fire. Of such things are friendships made.

About an hour later, we were only just containing the fire when one of the water-bearing planes came over and we all stood and gazed upwards as seawater rained down from the heavens. Trees hissed and popped and crackled, flames died and then erupted again as the plane flew off in the direction of Cala Llonga to pick up fresh supplies. The seaplane made several more trips to fill its tanks with water and then, as it made one more 'bombing raid', as suddenly as the fire had started, it gave up. The flames died completely and Tom and I were drenched in seawater one last time. It was as though we had received a benediction, for at that moment, the moon appeared through the smoke over the hill behind Tom's house and we knew the battle had been won. Smoke continued to drift upwards for another 24 hours and we all took turns to keep an eye on the hillside, but the fire had lost on this occasion.

An hour or so later, the weary fire-fighters had assembled on Tom's terrace and their families were putting together a celebratory breakfast. I was talking quietly to Katherine and some other neighbours when our Ibicencan friends raised a glass to make a *brindis*, a toast, to *amistad*, to friendship whatever the nationality. It's one of the wonderful aspects of the Ibicenco character. They just seem to absorb people into their island home in the most generous way. I doubt it if there was anywhere that was as integrated as Ibiza.

As I went to join in the toast, I raised my arm to wipe my mouth. I became aware that my skin smelled of pine smoke and herbs that grew wild on the hillsides, and I felt that finally I had become part of Ibiza.

෨

Later that night, we ended up in the sea that lapped against what had become known among the English as Pebble Beach. Famous for its football-sized rocks that had been worn smooth by the sea, the beach had become known for providing a number of residents with stones which they painted and sold through tourist shops to visitors. The beach shelved quite steeply but then it levelled off and the water retained the warmth of the day for some distance. I can't remember who suggested it but half a dozen of us had gone to the beach with a few bottles of wine and some food. We wanted to wash away the traces of our efforts from earlier in the evening and as we dived in, the moon reached the rim of the sea. Shards of moonlight shot across the surface of the water, broken into fragments by the ripples. We all waded ashore and opened the bottles. The panic of the evening had been replaced by lethargy and as we munched on a feast of fresh bread, *Manchego* cheese, *salchicha, jamon Serrano*, olives and grapes, the talk became quieter and quieter until, like so many dormice, we dozed. The night air was as warm and soft as velvet and the dried seaweed at the back of the beach made a perfect mattress.

An hour later, we all woke and went for one last swim. As we entered the water, we became aware of phosphorescence in the water. Our bodies were cloaked in fire and as we swam out to sea, so a different kind of fire followed us. Ibiza had surprised us yet again.

10.
Storm Damage

Gradually the long, hot summer days faded into autumn. When you dived into the sea to a depth of 15 to 20 feet, you were aware of a change in the sounds. Where the water had moved slowly and languorously during the summer, suddenly it had come alive. Fish darted around purposefully and there was a continual crackling and popping, as though you had dived into the middle of a bottle of chilled champagne. Looking back up at the surface where there'd been a mirror-like glassiness during the hot months, now it was agitated with small waves hurrying past as though they had an appointment on the beach. I'd gone to Es Pou d'es Llou for the last swim of the summer but the water really was too cold and I decided to dry off and head for the *pension*. When I got there, I found that a hissing butane heater had arrived in the corner of the dining room and the menu had changed. The food was heavier, with soups and *estofados* the order of the day, followed by cinnamon coffee.

Because of my experience of Ibiza during the winter months, I had quickly realised that efficient heating was essential. The one drawback to my house was the fact that it didn't have a working chimney. At first, along with much of the island, I bought a butane stove but while this heated the air, it didn't heat the walls. At the same time, it emitted large amounts of moisture which meant that you could easily end up with damp running down the walls and windows. This didn't make for a cosy way of life and it encouraged mould to grow on the lime-washed walls.

My second move was to install a cast iron wood-burning stove that could be loaded with olive, almond or pine logs. With its stovepipe chimney that disappeared up through the ceiling, it resembled something from the Wild West but it certainly did the trick. Leaving the trap closed at night meant that I could get up in the morning, give the remaining contents a stir, add some tinder and a dry log or two and within minutes, the house would be warm and, above all, dry.

Late one afternoon, I was sitting by the stove reading the *Diario de Ibiza*, with the radio burbling in the background. There was a smell of electricity and a feeling of foreboding in the air. Obviously a storm was brewing but nobody could have guessed what was actually going to happen. Given that diverting water from the flat roof and collecting it in the cisterna under the house was a major preoccupation for most residents, we always viewed a downpour as a heaven-sent and free opportunity to top up our water supplies. I went up onto the roof, swept it clear of twigs, branches and dust and then went back inside.

Like everybody else, I assumed the rain would be short and sharp and that, as usual, a minor river would run down the road near the house, making driving even more hazardous than usual. How wrong we were. The weird smell of static in the air got stronger and, as the light faded, the sky turned a horrible bruised yellowish colour and there was an unusual quiet in the valley. Not a leaf moved and the birds had taken shelter.

At about midnight, it started to rain. When you live in a place where water always needs to be conserved, the pleasurable anticipation of rain is overwhelming. You feel like a kid on the night before Christmas. Thunder and lightning roared and crashed around the valley and the usually welcome sound of water running down the pipe into the cisterna became disconcertingly noisy. By 2am, there had been no let up in either the celestial *son* or the *lumiere* and the rain was as hard as ever. I went outside onto the covered terrace with a book I happened to have in my hand. The lightning was so intense and continuous that it provided me with enough illumination to read quite easily. I went back inside and had a look in the cisterna. By now this was full and water was pouring down the six inch wide pipe, turning sharp left and disappearing out into the garden through the overflow.

With a thump and a crash, a large pine tree behind the house toppled over, taking with it a section of my garden wall. This in turn cleared a path for a miniature river to pour down past the house, bringing mud and a landslide of small stones. These then joined a much bigger torrent tumbling down what once had been the road. Finally, it poured down the valley and removed both the beach in its entirety leaving an enormous expanse of mud and, to the astonishment of the local residents, also a bulldozer that had been on the beach.

By 6am things had quietened down considerably. However, the volume of the rain had opened up a series of leaks in my roof. The water had wriggled and wormed its way through the grouting between the tiles on the flat roof, then down through the concrete layer over the concrete beams and seeped through the plaster until finally drips rained down in different rooms but especially in my bedroom. The worst was the one that fell neatly in the middle of my bed, but a series of buckets, tins and pans enabled me to catch a few hours sleep despite the musical plinking and sploshing. Thankfully I had a good supply of dry firewood in the house and this helped to keep the house reasonably damp free.

At midday, I decided to go into Ibiza town to see how everyone else had coped. Turning the car onto the back road over the hill that connected Ibiza and Santa Eulalia through the village of Jesus proved hopeless. There were simply too many rocks, stones and branches lying across the tarmac and the cross-country *caminos*, the unsealed country roads, were totally impassable. The depth of the trenches that water can carve out of dirt roads amazed me. The problem was that the soil baked hard during the summer heat and when rain did come, especially in the quantity of the previous night, it simply found its way down to the sea over land rather than sinking in and doing some good.

Finally, I managed to find a way through to the main road to Ibiza and was greeted by the astonishing sight of cars that had been picked up and dumped like children's toys by the side of the road. Trees lay on their sides like oversized matchsticks and everywhere were small collections of rubbish that miniature rivers had gathered up and then, becoming bored, had discarded at random. The dried-up riverbed spanned by the stone bridge into Santa Eulalia contained a roaring, bucking, foaming river of mud, bushes and rocks.

Once in town it was clear that the only topic being discussed in the bars was the storm. There were a few excited foreigners I'd met a couple of times before, all comparing how they'd got on. Time slipped by, as it had a habit of doing in Ibiza, and a couple of beers turned into lunch with a few friends in a restaurant located just behind the port area of town. Because of the weather, a number of items were missing from the menu but as we sat down at the green painted tables with their cheerful tablecloths, the smell of garlic, olive oil and onions was almost overpowering.

"*Bon dia, Señores,*" called out Juanita from behind the bar, "*buenos dias*. How are you all and how are your houses? *Unas gotitas de agua* inside, I believe, *si*? I think you need a *sopa de garbanzos y jamon*, the soup made with chickpeas and ham, to keep out the cold and a good bottle of *vino tinto*, strong red wine."

This was in the days before the market in Spanish wines exploded throughout the world, and what we drank most days was *vino corriente*, a house wine that cost seven pesetas a bottle and nobody asked any smart questions about whether it was corked. It couldn't have been, of course, because once you removed the small metal top, there was a neat little plastic cap which, if you were known in the restaurant, you could replace to save whatever you hadn't drunk and it would be put up on a shelf until the next time you came in. I once heard a particularly famous English theatrical knight exclaim at a dinner party what a wonderful vintage he had in his glass. I was slightly surprised as I'd seen our hostess decanting the *vino corriente* into antique decanters not an hour before he arrived. As she agreed with him, she turned to me with the broadest of smiles and winked. "My dear," she cried, "You've no idea how good it is."

On this particular day after the storm, none of us felt much like leaving any wine for another visit. It was still cold and damp outside and rumours had been flying round about possible casualties from the torrential rain and we were just glad to be safe in a warm and friendly place. Juanita quickly reappeared with baskets laden with fresh bread, bowls of olives, some of which were enormous with a garlic clove firmly inserted, and *ail-i-olli* which differed completely from the one I'd enjoyed so much in the summer. This one was thicker and more substantial, but with a slightly less tongue-melting strength.

The restaurant quickly filled up with a mix of nationalities. The vent in the window over the front door broadcast a hypnotic aroma of cooking which drew in a mix of Ibicencos, mainland Spanish, English, Dutch, Germans and French, who all retreated from the world outside to enjoy the wonderful food. A sprinkling of Americans were beginning to turn up on the island as the Vietnam war got worse and they were welcomed along with all the other nationalities that made Ibiza a mini-United Nations. Obviously, the common language was English, but a patchwork of different dialects, accents and languages wove together and somehow we all understood each other. Maybe the wine helped.

"Have you heard about the prison?" laughed a German girl called Helga who was sitting opposite me.

"No," I replied, "I didn't know there was one. What's happened?"

"Well, when you are sent to prison, you enter through double doors into a courtyard. Once you're inside, you have to find a cell that's empty and that's where you live. You can order whatever you want from a local restaurant and the food is sent in to you in a basket. Well, there's a rumour going round that an American smuggled word to friends working in a restaurant that he wanted a roast chicken and that they should inject it with LSD. So they did what he wanted and, as it was being delivered to the prison, the *commandante* saw it and demanded that it should be served to him immediately and he's been high for the last couple of days."

Our roar of laughter disturbed the restaurant's ginger tom which was asleep on a barstool. He jumped down, stretched and sauntered over for a tickle behind the ears and a quick hunt for any scraps that had fallen onto the floor.

"I've heard that the prison also has an honour system where you are released at the weekends but you have to promise to come back on the Monday morning," continued Dutch Rudi. "If any of the prisoners don't turn up, they send the others out to search for them."

By now we were halfway through our wonderful bowls of soup and the pace had slowed. Juanita had warned us that because of the storm the main menu was off and we'd eat whatever the chef was making. Some of us had ordered main courses and a *flan* for pudding and we were beginning to regret it as we filled up. But the beauty of the lifestyle was that the river of conversation flowed gently through the afternoon, and as our empty bowls were replaced with dishes of a local pasta recipe, nobody hurried us, nobody made us feel that we should leave the restaurant to make way for the next customers.

Eventually Juanita served the *flans* with their wonderful burned caramel sauce and coffees and cognacs. It was about 4.30pm and as a few hardy souls made their way back to the outside world, the remaining guests pulled their chairs up to join us. At the same time, Juanita and her husband Pepe came out and sat down with us to a round of applause.

"*Señores, amigos mios*" explained Pepe, "today we should all be grateful for friendship and for the food we have to eat. *Un brindis*, a toast, to friends." And as we all raised our glasses, the first faint rays of late afternoon sun peered apologetically and hesitantly through the glass doors as though they were embarrassed by the storm of the night before.

By late afternoon, I found my Seat 600 and wound my way towards Santa Eulalia even though the roads were still covered with stones, boulders, fallen trees and branches. Eventually I arrived home ready to begin the process of mopping up. Inside my front door there was a chicken and vegetable stew in a pot. A note simply said, "*Señor Eduardo, no sabia si Vd. tiene algo para comer. Sus vecino.*" This translated as "Dear Stewart, I didn't know if you have anything to eat. Your neighbour."

11.
A Great Lunch

Helga and Willi were a German couple who, at some stage in life had amassed quite a number of worldly goods. In addition, Helga had managed to gather quite a few pounds that had settled somewhere between her waist and her knees. She enjoyed life to the full and this included regular transfusions of vodka and tonics ("darling Villi won't know because vodka doesn't smell of alcohol"), buying jewellery and entertaining. It hardly needs pointing out that all of this meant spending considerable chunks of her husband's hard-earned cash.

Willi on the other hand was small and slim and resembled nothing so much as a Swiss gnome. Inside his head, however, lurked a brain that clearly had an aptitude for business. Having amassed a fairly hefty bank balance, that was exactly where he liked his money to stay and while he couldn't be described as mean, you could see that parting with hard cash was always a wrench for him. When he had to pay a bill, his face would take on the look of a mother having her children snatched from her. On the other hand, they were both charming, kind and always willing to enjoy life.

Before they plunged into buying the land to build their house outside Ibiza town, they found a foothold on the island's property ladder in the shape of an apartment in San Antonio. In those far-off days, San Antonio was pretty much a sleepy little fishing village where you could find a wonderful lunch or dinner for a handful of pesetas and the most excitement you'd have was deciding which bar to go to after eating and whether you should have a cognac or a glass of *hierbas*. Life was slow and sleepy and the thought of all-night raves, clubs and coach loads of tourists arriving in their hundreds had never crossed anyone's mind.

The apartment that Helga and Willi had bought was on the fifth floor in one of the first blocks to be built in town. Consisting of three bedrooms, two bathrooms and a rather primitive kitchen, the windows in the living room were set into bay alcoves and these gave a fine view over the bay. Although Willi was pretty pleased with it, for Helga it was clearly just a trial run, an ironing-out of the learning curve of property buying before she built her mini-castle-by-the-sea on the outskirts of Ibiza town.

Having completed the purchase, she set about changing almost every aspect of the apartment. Recently constructed walls were demolished, new ones were built, channels were hacked out of fresh plaster to accommodate new wiring and pipes, wardrobes were ripped out and new ones installed and furnishings arrived from Germany by the truck load.

I went to pick up my post one day from my local bar and delving through assorted letters, bills and notices I found a note from Helga summoning me to translate for her over what was obviously proving to be a thorn in her slightly voluminous side. "Dear Stewart," ran the missive, "Willi and I wish your helping with a problem. Please come sooner and we will also buy your lunch at the same time if not sooner. Yours, dear friend, Helga and Willi." I could have pretended that it never arrived but curiosity got the better of me and I set off across the island via San Rafael. From the road down into San Antonio I could just make out the apartment block and, as I wound my way through the narrow back streets, I wondered what the problem could be that their millions of deutchmarks couldn't solve. I doubted that it was anything that I could help with. The front door of the apartment was open and inside I could see a wide variety of plumbers, electricians and carpenters struggling to understand Helga's fractured Spanish.

For example, roughly translated she said to an electrician, "Make the light shining from the tap by the bathroom by the switch." I have to admit she said it with great confidence but

I could see that however good or bad my Spanish might be after three years in Spain, it had to be better than Helga's and I plunged in where I could. Fairly soon, I had a line of workmen in front of me all asking for solutions to problems that had been created specifically by her. Gradually I managed to sort things out and Helga stood next to me smiling in a fluffy sort of way and interjecting the occasional, "*Ja, gut.*" Each time she said it, a kind of communal seismic tremor was set off in the assembled representatives of the Spanish labour force.

By the time lunch came, there was a sort of general weariness and I felt this might be the time to suggest that we decamped and left our Spanish heroes to relax and recover from their labours. As all rich men do, Willi was clearly feeling the strain on his bank account as he totted up the cost of each mistake that Helga had made and his relief at having a relatively fluent Spanish speaker in his midst was reflected in a) his choice of restaurant and b) his choice of wine. I spotted a favourite of mine, Tondonia, on the wine list and Willi lashed out immediately. Not for him plastic caps on the top of bottles; for someone used to litre and a half bottles of *vino del campo*, this was heady stuff. Over the starter of *jamon serrano*, figs and thin slices of Manchego cheese we talked about their plans for the apartment and whether I could make a weekly trip over to San Antonio to ensure that things ran smoothly. Over the main course of *lechal*, suckling pig, potatoes roasted in their jackets in the embers of the fire and salad we discussed their plans for the house outside Ibiza town and over *crema Catalana* and ice cream, we talked about the future of the island and what the next 20 years would bring. By now, the Tondonia had taken hold and I had visions of being their site manager for something resembling the Hanging Gardens of Babylon. My finances took on an equally rosy glow and I felt that good things were definitely heading my way.

It was unfortunate that all of this was spoiled during the coffee by a banshee-like wail from Helga. "God in heaven," she cried frantically, "oh no, I am stupid voman." At this point Willi, obviously suspecting the worst, buried his face in his hands.

"Darling," he moaned, as more marks drained from his imagination and his wallet, "what now?"

"Yes," I found myself echoing like a Greek chorus that is expecting the worst, "what now?"

"I am forgetting I have speaking to Juan the carpenter about the day bed. I vos asked him to make it fit for the alcove by cutting off the legs and shortening it. He say it problem und I say do it someway and he say OK." Like the voice of doom, she added, "I wonder vot he has done."

By now, Willi had taken up the main theme and he repeated, "I too wonder vot he has done."

Lunch was clearly over and Willi called for the bill in the voice that had made him a force to be reckoned with in Munich's business community. We leapt in my car and sped back to the apartment. Parking near the front door, Helga and Willi jumped from the vehicle with surprising flexibility for two people bordering on their seventies.

I was winding up the driver's window when I heard a low moan combined with a screech that you'd normally only hear from a graveyard at midnight. As one, both protagonists cried in anguish, "What is that?" I climbed out of the car and followed their gaze upwards. Sticking out of the side wall of the alcove of their apartment were the two legs and the end of a once-elegant day bed. The whole thing had been neatly bricked and cemented in place and to cap it all, a seagull was perched happily on the once proud piece of furniture. Willi picked up a stone in fury and without any hope of hitting it hurled the rock at the offending bird. What he said is best left un-translated but suffice to say that Juan found himself unemployed, the apartment went back on the market in short order and the fact that I couldn't stop shaking with laughter meant that I went back to Santa Eulalia one extremely fine lunch to the good, but minus the job of site manager.

However, I kept in touch with Willi and Helga and they did build a splendid house and swimming pool outside Ibiza. It was some years later though, that Willi took up boats in a big way. He bought a 38-foot power boat, found himself a boatman, and whenever he was in Ibiza he could be seen at the Yacht Club buying ever-increasing amounts of electronic equipment designed to show him the sea bed lurking beneath his boat. He became an ardent fisherman and spend hours out on the water desperately hoping for an enormous catch. Actually, what he tended to bring back were small sharks that proved almost inedible. However, family and friends were frequently invited to Helga and Willi's table to enjoy shark and chips.

Thankfully the intrepid couple were away when their boat was lowered back into the water after having its bottom scraped and repainted. According to the story that went the rounds later on, what happened could have been avoided if one vital thing had been done. Perhaps the most pertinent point of the work that had taken place was that someone had forgotten to replace what can only be described as the bung.

Again I can only say that this is alleged, as I was not an eyewitness, but what seems to have happened was that the boat slipped neatly out of the slings once it was lowered and having come to rest in the water, it bobbed happily at first. Then however, it became apparent to onlookers that it seemed to be settling rather low in the water. In fact, it sank ever faster and it wasn't long before, with a dispirited gurgle that might well have been emitted by one of Helga's former workers, the boat disappeared beneath the murky waters of the harbour.

Eventually it was raised and drained of all the bits and pieces that boats collect when they spend a bit of time resting on the seabed, but I think for Willi, this was the seagull on the daybed of his dreams of catching a monster fish. He seemed to lose heart and soon he turned to golf. As for Helga, she was just relieved that she hadn't been responsible for the boat's untimely end and that her Willi was safe and sound. Of course, being the man he was, Willi had to have the latest clubs, every gadget that came on the market that promised him a perfect swing, and he spent hours on the course with the club professional in a vain attempt to become a world-class golfer. He never did become one – but he had a lot of fun trying.

12.
A Dining Car

A small house crouched on the edge of a field in a direct line with mine but about 50 feet below and on the other side of the dirt road. Built by a retired English couple called Ted and Irene, this was not what you might have called a desirable residence but they moved in and loved the place dearly. They were certainly eccentric and despite Ted labouring with the difficulty of having a speech problem that made his communicating in Spanish somewhat difficult, they seemed to enjoy each day.

Physically, they were total opposites. Ted was tall, thin and slightly stooped from his years working as a clerk in a post office and his movements were like an elderly heron, while Irene was short, plump and she moved as fast as a sparrow. They had a wonderful marriage, no shortage of money as far as anyone could tell and dreams that left the rest of the world standing.

I once went over to them for a drink and found Irene reading a volume on whale fishing in the 19th century while Ted was ploughing his way through his daily dose of Russian verbs. The chances of Irene going whale fishing or of Ted having the possibility of speaking Russian were less than slim, but they loved all kinds of challenges and they would talk with enormous enthusiasm about the most extraordinary ideas. "You never know, my dear," she would giggle, "you never know."

The house consisted of one bedroom, a bathroom, a small kitchen and a minute living room. Typical of houses that were built in Spain at that time, the tile floor was freezing cold most of the time and totally unforgiving if you dropped anything on it. Narrow terraces ran around two sides of the property, low arches shielded the rooms from any trace of daylight, the earth in the garden was absolutely solid and the view was almost non-existent.

The interior was simple apart from the startlingly-coloured paintings of frenetic flamenco dancers that decorated the walls. In the evening, they would turn on one overhead light wherever they were. If they were reading in the living room, the light would be on there. If they moved to the kitchen for dinner where they had a small table and two chairs, they would carefully turn out the living room light and turn on the one in the kitchen. This was because our valley didn't have electricity at that point. Instead, Ted and Irene had invested in a small and unreliable generator that needed the same care and attention as a patient in intensive care.

When Ted opened the front door, it was like looking into a mole's nest as he stood at the door blinking at the world outside. "Hello," he'd greet you, "come on in and I'll put the kettle on." He'd be wearing a thick cardigan and Irene would have a woollen shawl around her shoulders and they'd both be clutching hot drinks in their hands. As their first winter in Ibiza wore on, their enthusiasm seemed to be drooping and I noticed that they emerged less and less – they were obviously feeling the cold.

At that time, central heating simply wasn't available; the house never really warmed up on even the sunniest of days and for the first time, it seemed as though they were showing signs of their age. In the middle of the living room was a butane heater but they weren't strong enough to change the orange-coloured butane gas bottle and even when it was full, they never had more than one panel lit. "Don't like to trouble people too much," Ted would say. Neighbours changed the bottle as often as they could but things were looking bleak for our wonderful dreamers.

Ted and Irene owned a Citroen Diane, a car that was the slightly more up-market version of the Deux Chevaux. Even though the bodywork was a bit tougher, the suspension of the Diane was just as flexible and bouncy as the junior version. It was rather like having a steering wheel and a primitive motor attached to a waterbed. Additionally, the windows didn't have a winding mechanism. Instead, they were hinged across the middle and you folded them up to the open position and down to close it.

Doubtless Ted was a safe and proper driver at home in his native East Anglia but in Europe he swooped from one side of the road to the other with an abandon that swallows would have envied. Drivers and pedestrians scattered in every direction but Irene seemed to gain enormous pleasure from the way Ted drove, crying out with delight as they went on their way.

The day came when Ted and Irene solved the problem of their fridge-like home in their own way. The Citroen used to sit hunched in their driveway when it wasn't terrorising other road users. One morning I was on my terrace enjoying the first rays of the early morning sun when there was the sound of Ted and Irene's car doors opening and shutting. I waited for the unmistakable sound of the Citroen starter motor that resembled a giant slowly grinding large pieces of metal together. A whirring sound would creep into the grinding and finally, reluctantly, the engine would stir itself into life.

The only noise I heard, however, was of Ted whistling cheerfully as he went back into the house. This was unusual enough these days but I presumed he had forgotten something and about ten minutes later, out he came again. The car door opened and closed and once more there was perfect silence. Finally I couldn't resist having a look and so I peered cautiously through the railings. I parted the geranium leaves and suddenly I could see what they were doing. There they sat, side by side on the front seat of the car, a tray laden with breakfast in front of each of them. And the wonderful thing was that the car was facing the sun. It must have been toast warm and I sank back onto my seat with relief, marvelling at how inventive they had been.

For the rest of the day, I stayed on my terrace as much as I could and kept peering through my plants to see that they were safe and not suffering from sunstroke. Ted took the dirty dishes into the house when they'd finished breakfast and re-appeared a while later with books and magazines and there they sat for the rest of the morning.

Lunchtime came and it was Irene's turn to go in to the house. She prepared the food and out she came out with the trays, a bottle of wine and a couple of glasses. Ted opened the window on his side of the car and Irene handed in his lunch. An hour later, with the dishes cleaned and tidied away, Irene carefully pulled small floral patterned curtains that she had arranged on a wire around the side windows and across the windscreen, and they settled down for a siesta.

In the early evening I took a bottle of wine and went over to see them. I felt awkward about mentioning that I knew how they had spent the day but Irene was bubbling with happiness when I told her I'd seen them in the car. "There you are," she cried, giggling happily, "come on in, dear. We've had the most wonderful day and we're so lovely and warm. Wasn't it a good idea? We were driving into town the other day and Ted was a bit on the wrong side of the road if you know what I mean – and I noticed how lovely it was with the sun shining in the window. Ooh, look here, let's get that cork out. Do sit down. I want to tell you about the book I'm reading about trekking in Mongolia. Now that's something I'd like to try. Wouldn't you Ted?"

"*Da, da,*" he replied, his Suffolk accent altering the words so much that no Russian would have realised he was agreeing with Irene.

Day after day for as long as the cold weather lasted the pair would repeat the same manoeuvres of living in their car during the day. They proudly showed me how Irene had made neat little tiebacks for the curtains and Ted had fashioned supports for the trays that clipped onto the dashboard. One day they invited me to lunch and I was ushered into the back seat. A tray with a glass of wine and a plate of fish and chips was placed on my lap and there we sat happily munching away and chatting about climbing in the Rockies and whether Ted should think about switching from Russian to Swahili. He felt that the verbs might be a problem. "I'm not getting very far with Russian. There's nobody to chat to. On the other hand, you may have noticed," he explained, "that I have a slight speech problem and I've heard that in Swahili they do this clicking business with their tongues in their language. I'm not sure I could click very well."

Some years passed and one day I answered a knock on the front door to find Ted and Irene practically bouncing up and down with excitement. "We wanted you to be the first to know. We've had enough of living in the old car almost every day, and now that electricity has arrived in the neighbourhood, we've bought a piece of land up the valley and we're going to build a new house. We're going to have heating and lots of lights and shelves full of books."

Finally the day came when the builders, the plumbers and plasterers, the painters and the electricians moved out. The house was ready and Ted and Irene moved in. I found a note that had been slipped under my front door inviting me to be the first person to visit them in their new home. They wanted me to come at 7pm so that I could admire the sun going down behind the hill on the other side of the valley and enjoy their new lights.

I arrived punctually and they opened the front door to let me into a blaze of colour. One wall of the living room was painted a deep and vibrant red while the adjoining wall was a rich royal blue. The other two walls were the rather more normal white and in the middle of the room hung an enormous chandelier. It was so low that anybody taller than five foot six inches was in danger of being scalped. "We had it hung especially low so that we've lots of light for reading in the evenings," explained Ted. "Hang on a sec, I'll turn it on so you can get the full effect. This is the first time, mind, and we wanted you to be here when we did."

As he peered around the room, a puzzled look appeared on his face. "Just a minute, I'll be back in a second." He disappeared into the kitchen, then he went upstairs and Irene and I heard him moving from room to room. Eventually he came back down looking furious. "What's the problem, Ted?" I asked.

"Well," he replied, "you see they've wired in the lights and the power points?"

"Yes, dear," replied Irene. "What of it?"

"The buggers have forgotten to include switches. We'll have to get the generator out again until they do."

13.
Testing Time

By now the time had come for me, along with a large number of residents, to take a Spanish driving test. Under an agreement between the two governments, we'd been allowed to drive on our own national licences, but bureaucracy had finally caught up with us. Obviously the process had to be discussed at some length and this meant that residents gathered in small groups in bars the length and breadth of the island to swap the latest gossip about how terrible it was all going to be. And, of course, it would have been terrible because living on Ibiza at that time without a *Permiso de Conducir*, a Driving Licence, would have been almost impossible.

"Have you heard," I was asked one day in Angie's Bar by an exceptionally serious British expat, "not only are we going to have to take a driving test, we're also going to have to undergo a thorough medical as well. I mean to say, I wouldn't have allowed my wife to have to put up with such a thing in Kenya and I'm not going to put up with it here." And with that he tucked an imaginary swagger stick under his arm and strode out into the street as though he was going to face the enemy.

On the other hand, Angie giggled sexily, leant across the bar displaying two sumptuous advantages and murmured, "I wouldn't mind a medical from that divine *medico* on the Via Punica." In fact, the number of women who suddenly needed the signature of a doctor on a variety of forms testified to the attractions of the new Doctor.

By the time we had all filled in the forms and sent them off to Palma via a *Gestor*, a kind of legal hack, a somewhat soggy and bleary-eyed spring had arrived on the island. "I can't remember a wetter April," was the cry. "We might just as well be back in England," exclaimed the foolish ones who had forgotten what life was like back across the Channel.

Eventually, we were all summoned to a bar on the outskirts of Ibiza town on a day when the gods had decided that what Ibiza really needed was an extra layer of mud thanks to the monsoon-like rain. The bar was located near the football ground and set in a vague rectangle of roads and this was to be the testing ground for our hopeful drivers.

We had been summoned for 9am and despite knowing that this meant we'd probably not be needed until about 11am, nevertheless a large number arrived at the bar at the appointed time, so keen were we all to obtain that precious piece of paper that said we were legally allowed on the roads.

Unfortunately, a number of factors coincided. These were 1) that it was freezing cold, 2) that it was still extremely damp, 3) that the bar was open when we all arrived and 4) the only shelter was inside the hostelry. While it should have been obvious that this way led to disaster, we congregated around the bar, bought our various drinks and clustered around the only butane heater in the place. More and more hopefuls arrived and followed our example and at about 10am, we realised that our tester and his merry men had not arrived from Palma but a fair old party was in progress.

Half an hour later, however, a stir outside indicated that we should all appear stone cold sober and present ourselves in reasonably good order. We lurched outside and found a particularly small man with an assistant who also seemed to be a translator of sorts. For some reason he decided to move the Seat 600 in which he had arrived even though it wasn't particularly blocking the way. He started up the engine, threw the gear lever into reverse. The car shot backwards and with a clang, it smacked into a boulder by the side of the road. Our tester greeted us cheerfully.

"*Buenos dias, damas y caballeros*," cried the small man.

"Good day, lady and gentleman," called out the assistant.

"*Yo soy el encargado por este examen para el Permisso de Conducir.*"

"I am making you testing for...for...*el Permisso de Conducir,*" finished the echo somewhat lamely.

"*Por favour, los nombres.* Plis, names."

Those of us who had been the earliest arrivals started to have fits of the giggles and this infected large parts of the crowd so our brave official was confronted by 50 or 60 foreigners all heaving with suppressed laughter. One or two had already drifted back into the bar, but the rest of us stood our ground and called out our names. Our hero, the tester, became totally confused and demanded that we should all start again.

I spotted a friend called Irena lurking on the other side of the crowd with her boyfriend, an Englishman called Frank who'd started a leather shop in town. They were clearly trying to register their names and as I'd already managed to log mine with our minute official, I went across and offered to help. Finally, we all received times 15 minutes for our test, and given the state of the ground, which had turned into something resembling an Amazonian swamp, we all congregated indoors to compare times.

I had to wait until 11.45am before my date with destiny and so I found a corner of the bar that was relatively empty and retired with a drink and a copy of the *Diario de Ibiza*, which I hoped would help my burgeoning attempts to speak *Castilian*, the official language of Spain.

Finally my time came and I went outside. Unfortunately the rain had made the already muddy road into an absolute quagmire and in my attempt to step across a puddle, I slipped and fell backwards into the mud and water. My life flashed before my eyes as I had visions of drowning while taking a driving test but friendly hands pulled me up and despite my unattractive condition, I was bowed into the car by the assistant who resembled an usherette showing me to my seat in a cinema.

I slid behind the steering wheel and shook hands with the tester. He in turn giggled at me in the friendliest fashion and asked me to take off the handbrake, to press down on the clutch and see if the car would start.

It was clear from the quantity of water on the road that the motor must have been getting pretty wet, but I pressed down on the clutch, turned the key in the ignition and the engine chugged into life. Releasing my foot from the clutch caused the vehicle to shoot forward as I clutched frantically at the wheel. My companion beamed all over his face as he made a mark against a form on his clipboard that rested on his extra large briefcase. "*Muy bien, Señor, muy bien.* You are excellent at making the starting of the car. The waiting is making it not work very well. Now, please proceed straightway."

To proceed straightway was virtually impossible given the liquid state of the road and I weaved in and out of the deeper holes. However, I seemed to satisfy my friend in the passenger seat even though the foot brake failed to work most of the time. We skidded our way around the course and as we arrived outside the bar once more, I managed to slow down the car by aiming it at a particularly nasty puddle. It was rather like hitting a wall. The car shuddered and jolted to a halt and a wave of mud sloshed up onto the bonnet.

I thought I was bound to have failed the test but my small companion let out a cry of delight. "*Señor, enhorabuena*, congratulations. You have passed the test." This was all said in an incomprehensible Spanish but thankfully the assistant had stuck his head in the window and was able to explain to me what was being said. I shook hands with the tester, thanked him profusely and stepped out of the vehicle. I decided I needed one more drink and I as entered the bar, an amazingly attractive and wealthy Englishwoman called Lynda came tottering out. "Hello darlings," she cried, her jewellery clanking and jingling as she lurched over to the car. "Are you ready for me?" Clearly she'd drunk most of the bar dry and I decided that maybe I should get back into town.

About a week later, I bumped into her in the Via Punica as she emerged from a *Gestor*. "Darling, darling" she tinkled loudly, "where did you get to after taking your driving test, you old spoilsport?" She stroked my arm in a rather affectionate manner.

"Oh I had things to do," I replied hastily. "How did you get on?"

"Well," she giggled happily, "I passed. I've just been in to pick up my new licence."

"What?" I asked somewhat rudely, "you passed?"

"Yes, but on the other hand, in his condition, he had to pass me."

"What condition?" I couldn't think what she meant.

"Darling, I suggested we should have a drink or two after I'd driven that delicious little car. You don't imagine he was going to fail me by the time we left the bar, do you? Now then," she went on flirtatiously, "why don't we go and celebrate our new licences – or our licentiousness?"

14.

Horsing Around

I'd been in Ibiza for about three years when I fell deeply and irrevocably in love. The object of my passion had large, dark, moist eyes, the most attractive ears and a delicate, *retroussé* nose. She also had four of the most gorgeous legs imaginable and a temperament, when she chose, that wouldn't have upset a dormouse. On occasion, though, she could let fly like a prima donna in full flood.

Adelfa was a two-year-old, 14 hands Arabian filly. I originally clapped eyes on one of her relatives at the annual Arab Horse Show in Madrid. The owner of this particular horse was Don Rafael, with a title and a pedigree as long as that of his horses and, as it turned out, an enormous *cortijo* in Andalucia. It was one of Adelfa's proud parents who was prancing happily around the show ring; one thing led to another and I found myself being invited to his home to see the rest of the stable.

Having returned home to Ibiza to think things over, I eventually decided to take up his offer. After all, just going and seeing the horses wasn't going to commit me to anything. I could always say no, couldn't I? At that time the military used to send stallions from a wide variety of breeds around the country so that owners of mares could breed them with a stallion of a certain quality. My vision of the future was of purebred Arab foals carrying on Adelfa's line, with her as the matriarch of the herd.

I put my car on the ferry to Alicante and some hours later the boat docked in what seemed to be a city of palm trees. Dinner beckoned before setting off in the direction of Andalucia. In those days there weren't any motorways or *peajes*, tollgates, and the roads were in poor condition, therefore it seemed pretty obvious I wouldn't be able to get any refreshment on the way, so having dinner before setting off made a lot of sense.

In a small back street I found a restaurant with a terrace full of Spanish families. That's always a good enough recommendation, so I settled down with a road map while I waited for the menu. It seemed best to head for Granada and then on to Malaga. At this point the waiter arrived and to save time I asked for a bottle of Tondonia, that most wonderfully dark red, almost black, wine, a bowl of chilled *gazpacho* soup, *ail-y-olli* and crusty bread, a main course of *sepia* in its ink followed finally by a flan.

It's so satisfying sitting at a portside restaurant in the early evening. The heat of the day lingers in the pavement and the walls, the amazing pearly light lasts for about 30 minutes at that latitude, and as you sip a delicious wine and eat good food, it makes you just want to linger on and on. The Keats phrase, "A drowsy numbness pains my senses," just about described how I felt. However, I knew I had to set off and head west and so taking with me a bottle of water from the restaurant, I climbed into my car. I wound my way out of the city and headed off into the sunset. As the night wore on, I passed through the ghostly and desolate landscapes of Murcia and the sleeping villages round the Costa Blanca, all lit by an enormous moon that cast a weird light on the countryside. Finally at about 4.30am, I arrived outside Granada railway station. Needless to say, in a major Spanish city such as this, there was always going to be a bar open 24 hours a day and so I parked and went in.

The coffee machine was spluttering and steaming on one end of the bar, a large group of *habitués* were grouped around the other end and the cacophony of noise was deafening. A few people were sitting at tables reading the first editions of the local newspapers and over everything hung a pall of cigarette smoke. The owner's wife came out of the kitchen with a delicious looking plate of *tortilla Española*, Spanish omelette, for a patron as well as a glass of beer, and all this in the middle of the night.

It seemed as though quite a few of the customers were probably railway workers and were either waiting to go on, or had just come off their shift. Depending which way round, they were either having dinner or breakfast. I ordered a *carajillo*, those tiny black coffees topped up with a cognac and a glass of water. With it, I had a Spanish version of a *croque monsieur* toasted sandwich. This consisted of two slices of fried bread wrapped round slices of *jamon serrano* and some form of local cheese and it tasted fantastic. I realised how my digestion had changed in my time in Ibiza. In England, I'd quite often not bother with breakfast, have a sandwich by mid-morning, very often skip lunch or have a hurried pint in a pub with probably another sandwich, and then have a large dinner at about seven in the evening.

In Spain I rarely started the day without an *ensaimada* and a *carajillo*. I might have an apple, one of the sugar-laden oranges with extraordinarily loose skins at midday or, if I were near a market, a bag of figs. Lunch would be in a bar and would be anything from a piece of chicken, plus a salad and crusty bread or potatoes, to a plate of pasta, a litre bottle of wine and a flan. Dinner would be fish, potatoes and a green vegetable or something similar, more wine, possibly more fruit, and a coffee and cognac. And yet I was consistently slim, I never gained a pound in weight and diet was something I never thought about. On the whole, the food was simply better quality than back in England, it certainly had more flavour and you never hurried over it. Your digestion was able to take its time and, like many people, I drank large quantities of water. This was before the era in England where people walk around the streets clutching minute bottles of water for which they have paid large amounts of cash.

After about an hour, I set off once again in the direction of Malaga. Behind me the sun rose in my driving mirror. It seemed to set fire to the whole horizon as dawn burst like an explosion over the sleeping land. More and more traffic came towards me as another day got underway and finally I arrived on what is now known the world over as the Costa del Sol.

Don Rafael had given me directions for when I arrived in Malaga. I simply had to turn right and drive north through the Montes de Malaga until I came to Antequera. I then had to continue for about another ten minutes until I arrived at the sign to his *cortijo*. The day had become searingly hot, the drive had been long and I booked into a nearby hotel. From a distance, the building appeared to be wearing an enormous purple hat and a fringe and it wasn't until I drew up in front of it that I realised that whole of the front and much of the roof were covered in the most glorious bougainvillaea.

My room was typical Spain in the early '70s. Dark, heavy furniture, religious paintings featuring legions of fed-up looking angels, beds that guaranteed instant backache the minute you lay down, and those awful narrow bolster pillows that gave northern Europeans an immediate, raging neck-ache. The shower was a close relative of a garden hose and you had no control whatsoever over the temperature. But the hotel had two things going for it. It had charming staff who ran an immaculate bar, outside was a gin-clear swimming pool and as I didn't have to be at Don Rafael's until six o'clock, I changed hurriedly, collected a beer and went for a swim. Lunch led into a siesta and I eventually dressed for my date with a horse.

The long driveway led me to a stand of tall trees, a high white wall and two enormous wooden doors. These were standing open and I peered into a marble flagstone covered courtyard. Dotted in a regular pattern were citrus trees with their trunks painted white with lime and in the far corner stood a marble horse trough.

Having rung a large bell that hung on an iron chain outside the front door, I stood and inhaled the perfume from the orange and lemon blossoms. Suddenly the door swung open and a butler in tails greeted me. Immaculately dressed apart from his trousers which were tucked into a pair of grubby Wellingtons, he ushered me into a dark hall filled with wonderful old oak furniture and told me that he would announce my arrival. I noticed that his hands were somewhat grubby for a man in his particular profession but I guessed he'd been doing something in the kitchen when I rang the bell. As I waited, an assortment of dogs came and inspected me. Clearly I passed muster as they all lay down and expected a tummy rub and a tickle behind the ears. Forgetting where I was for a moment, I knelt down and gave them all due care and affection until I heard Don Rafael's voice saying, "*Amigo mio*, you are a true Englishman. Dogs should always be given the attention they ask for and when they ask for it. Welcome to my house! My wife will join us in a few minutes. Why don't we go outside and watch the horses come in for their evening drink?" Rafael dressed more like an Englishman than a Spaniard. In other words he looked slightly country shabby. His English was also far better than my Spanish.

And so, surrounded by a swirl of canine admirers, we went back out to the marble terrace. A table had been set up under an umbrella and comfortable seats beckoned, as did a frosted ice bucket that contained a bottle of very cold and very good white wine. His wife Fifi, who I had met in Madrid, tall, slim and elegant in silk, came out and after greeting me settled down in a chair. "I love this moment," she laughed quietly. "Every evening I like to sit here and watch our babies." Almost as though on cue, another tall door was opened by the butler and delicately picking their way, in came a number of the most beautiful horses I had ever seen. They were predominantly pale grey with dark manes and tails, glorious dished faces and delicately pricked ears.

They made their way over to the marble trough I'd spotted when I arrived and without any pushing or shoving, they gathered round to drink. After a few moments of silence, Rafael and Fifi beckoned me to walk over with them to greet their 'babies'. The horses had been out in the fields all day as their dusty hooves showed. They obviously felt as I had when I arrived at my hotel and spotted a cold beer. The trough had an automatic filling system and this came on, ensuring that they had plenty to drink. Finally their owner pushed his way in between them and took the head collar of one of the most beautiful of the young horses. He led her round and round, talking to her like a lover.

"This is the filly I was talking about, Adelfa, aren't you my sweet one, eh? She has the *temperamento de una angelita*, like them all. You are all my babies," he whispered in her ear, "but you, darling, are very special. Tomorrow we will meet in the campo, in the fields where the *señor Ingles, Señor* Stewart will have a chance to watch you in your element and to admire you. And if he likes you, he might want to take you home with him." As he talked, he caressed her muzzle, gently pulling her ears and stroking her neck. He released her and Ramón the butler went and opened the door once more. He clicked his tongue, making that extraordinary noise in the cheek that obviously sounds so comforting to horses and the small herd made its way back out to the stable yard. It was all like a performance in the theatre and I was stunned by the beauty of the creatures I had met.

Throughout dinner Rafael, Fifi and I discussed little else other than Adelfa. I loved the fact that my dinner was served by Ramón whose only concession to the fact that he was handling food was to put on white cotton gloves and to change his boots for a pair of black shoes. By the time I left late that night I badly wanted to see Adelfa out of the artificial surroundings of the marble courtyard, but also I was longing to take her home to Ibiza with me. Back at the hotel, I had a swim in the pool. When I was an actor on a national tour of *Great Expectations*, I'd gone with the company to the local swimming pool in Manchester where the stage manager had taught me how to dive and to float and this particular night I put the latter skill to good use. I lay back in the warm water and gazed up at the stars and wondered if I was being completely mental in even considering the purchase of such a valuable and delicate creature. Would I know enough to care for her, would she settle down away from her family, was my plan to breed Arab horses totally crackpot? "Probably," I said to myself, "but let's see what happens tomorrow." And with that, I went to my room and tried to sleep on the dreadful bed.

The following morning when I opened my eyes, I had a neck-ache from the pillow and a tingle of excitement about going back to the *cortijo* and seeing Adelfa again. Pulling back the bedroom curtains revealed a cloudless blue sky that held the promise of a scorching day. I decided to go back to the pool for a quick swim and then I went off to the dining room for breakfast. This was something of a mistake. It consisted of slightly stale slices of country bread, a tired croissant, a plate of rubbery cheese and pre-formed ham and a basket of those horrible little plastic containers of various over-sugared jams and almost rancid butter. There were also two of those small, dome-shaped cakes called *Madalenas* which usually taste completely artificial and which I left completely alone. To drink, there was burnt-tasting coffee or tasteless tea bags and lukewarm water. Breakfast was not a success and I yearned for the bar at Granada Station.

About an hour later, I set off for the *cortijo*. Once again, Ramón opened the door for me. Now he was dressed in a rather more casual manner and led me through to dining room where Rafael and Fifi were clearly finishing a delicious breakfast that might well have come from Harrods or Fortnum & Mason. The house was redolent of bacon and eggs and wonderful toast and I was as jealous as I could be. "*Que tal*, Stewart, how are you? Looking forward to seeing the babies again, hmm? We've found this picture of Adelfa taken when she was very young." Rafael wiped his hands on his wife's linen napkin and handed me a photograph of a gangly, leggy, adorable looking foal peering wonderingly at the camera while her mother stood protectively behind her as though the cameraman was going to abduct her offspring.

"Now, let's go out to the fields and meet the horses again," he continued.

We went out through a series of dark corridors with paintings of horses decorating the walls until we came to the back door. Outside the sun hit me like a sledgehammer and Rafael ducked back inside to fetch me a large floppy hat. "*Hombre*, in this kind of heat, you need protection against the sun, especially for the head and back of the neck."

In the distance, I could see the herd of horses and a couple of people on horseback. My host waved his arm and called out to one of them. It had obviously been arranged that they would cut Adelfa out of the herd and bring her over on a leading-rein to where we were standing. This gave me the perfect opportunity to watch her moving. She was small, around 14 hands but her action was perfect daisy cutter, with her hooves swinging in a relaxed motion just above the ground.

She came to a stop just in front of us and let out a sort of 'brrrrrrh' as she breathed out with a snort. I'd come armed with a packet of mints that she had clearly smelled as her delicate little muzzle was exploring my sleeves, the front of my shirt and my trouser pockets. Taking out the packet, I put one of the mints in the palm of my hand. She let out a huge sigh of contentment and with the most delicate of nibbles, retrieved the treat. Adelfa stood there, looking as though she was thinking beautiful thoughts as she crunched her way happily through the mint. Within seconds she resumed the exploration but by now, the rest of the herd had come cantering up to see if any were left for them. An unseemly bout of pushing and shoving took place until they were shooed away again by Rafael. Adelfa stayed however, and I just stood there drinking in her beauty. Needless to say, I couldn't resist her and over lunch, I struck a deal with my host.

It was arranged that I would drive back to Ibiza and await a call from him. A travelling box would be built and I would accompany her in the wagon of a train that I was promised would only take about 16 hours to get to Alicante. There we would embark on a ferry and in no time at all we would be back in Ibiza.

15.

Fire in the Hearth

B ack home in Ibiza I ran into my taxi driver friend Antonio who had looked after me so well in my early days on the island. As I disembarked from the boat in my car, I spotted him waiting for a passenger. I parked illegally by the Customs House on the port and walked over to have a chat with him.

"Have you time for *una copa, Señor?*" he asked eagerly as we shook hands.

"But what about your clients?" I asked, pointing at the line of passengers who were clambering slowly down the gangplank from the ferry.

"*Es mas importante tomar una copa con un amigo, Señor. I* prefer to go and have a drink with a friend," he grinned and with that he locked his taxi and we went and settled ourselves on the terrace of a nearby restaurant. Two bottles of beer and a dish of salted almonds appeared as though by magic and Antonio turned the conversation to where I had been. I told him about my trip and how I was bringing back to Ibiza an exceptional example of an Arab horse.

"*Caray,*" he exclaimed, "Heavens, she sounds wonderful. I have always had a passion for horses, but an Arab mare. This is like the Queen coming to visit. You know, I have a *finca*, a farm, near Santa Gertrudis. If you ever need stables to keep her in the campo while you are away or for her to have a *vacacion*, a holiday, I would be honoured to look after her."

"*Gracias, amigo mio*, thank you so much for the offer," I replied. "I won't forget. What I need at the moment though is for someone to build me a chimney. I want to move the wood-burning stove into my bedroom and to have a proper chimney in my living room. Do you know any good builders?"

"Not a problem, *Señor* Eduardo, I know two or three. All I have to do is find out which one is free at the moment and I'll let you know." We finished our drinks and he went off to work while I went home.

A couple of days later Antonio appeared at the house late one afternoon. "*Hola, amigo mio,*" he called from the terrace. I went out carrying a bottle of white wine and a couple of glasses and after shaking hands, we sat in the shade. I had brought back from the mainland some exceptional *jamon serrano* and some olives stuffed with anchovies and I put these between us on a small table. The valley stretched away into the distance and the cicadas were tuning up for their evening concert. "Not such a bad life," laughed Antonio, as I poured the wine.

I had to agree with him when I thought about how I was when we first met and how dramatically things had changed for me. He went on, "The summer is normally a good time to find a builder, but this year everybody is busy. I don't know who I can recommend. I very sorry, *Señor,* I feel very bad in not knowing."

"Don't worry Antonio, I'll ask around Santa Eulalia and see if anyone can recommend a trustworthy chimney builder."

We sat and enjoyed the rest of the bottle and eventually Antonio left, reminding me once again about his *finca* if ever I needed help with Adelfa.

A couple of days later I was in the bar on the road into Santa Eulalia telling the owner Jaume about the problem I was having finding a chimney builder. "Well," he said, polishing his gold rimmed glasses, "there is always Pep. He says he's built a lot of things – I've never seen anything he's done but I could send him round to see you and you could judge for yourself."

"Wonderful," I thanked him, "I'll let you know what happens."

Two weeks later, I was making breakfast when there was a crash from outside on the terrace. Putting my head out of the front door, I found a small Ibicenco with an engaging smile picking up a table he'd knocked over. "*Buenas tardes, Señor, me llamo Pep*. I am friend of Jaume from the bar. I am builder first class *y muy excelente*."

An hour later we had agreed a price and a design for the chimney and he promised to start the following Monday. I went and bought the materials he said we required and needless to say, he turned up two weeks later than promised but at least I now had a builder. To my surprise and despite his age, Pep turned out to be a man of considerable energy. Work proceeded at enormous speed and my house was filled with the sound of hammering and drilling. Small gritty footprints appeared throughout the house where Pep's rope-sandaled *espadrilles* had brought in cement and sand but a quick sweep over the tiled floor soon dealt with the problem. Where the chimney for the wood-burning stove previously had gone through the roof, there appeared a much larger hole. In rapid succession, the stove was moved into my bedroom, and Pep started work on the base of the fireplace. His work was neat and tidy and the chimney-breast seemed to appear as if by magic.

I'd noticed that Pep seemed to work better in the mornings. It was pretty obvious that during his lunch he tended to drink a certain amount of red wine and once or twice he failed to return in the afternoon. But it didn't appear to affect the job, and within a remarkably short space of time, it was finished.

Once the cooler weather arrived, I invited a gaggle of friends plus Pep round for a ceremonial lighting of the new chimney. Beforehand though, I went off to the wood yard on the main Ibiza-Santa Eulalia road. Here you parked your car as near as possible to where the tree trunks were cut up and watched for the really choice wood to appear on the pile of logs. Large flat wicker baskets with a handle on either side were provided and the idea was to grab as many of the baskets as possible, fill them with your chosen wood, drag them to the man who was taking the cash and then pull them back to your car. It was a nice problem calculating how much the vehicle could hold. I once filled an early Citroen Diane I owned with so much wood that I did something irreparable to its suspension and it died a broken-backed, sad and much-lamented death.

The weather was really still too warm for a fire but I felt like an overexcited child and I thought we could open the windows wide once it was alight. On arriving at the wood yard, I found that they were cutting wonderful almond and olive logs. Both are slow and hot burning and they don't spit like pine. I edged my car past those of the other people waiting for wood until I was near Pierre's rather smart BMW. An elegant Frenchman who always wore extremely chic clothes, I couldn't believe he would sully his *voiture* with horrid things like logs, but I quickly spotted him clambering over a miniature mountain of wood like a gazelle, choosing good, solid logs and rejecting the dross. I feared for his incredibly expensive, soft leather Bally loafers. "*Ah mon ami,*" he cried when he saw me, "the hunt is on for *les meilleurs* logs."

As fast as I could, I filled the baskets, had them weighed and then loaded them into the back of an elderly Renault 4 I had bought. Soon the car was fully laden and I wandered over to where Pierre was just closing the boot of the BMW. "Stewart, my friend, you don't have a chimney and those logs are too big for your wood-burning stove. What is afoot, my dear friend?"

I explained about Pep and the official lighting. "Pep will be there, plus about 15 others. Why don't you come and have a drink?"

"I would not miss it for *le monde*. I shall be there at seven o'clock with a large log in my hands." He gave me a slow and distinctly rude wink and reversing the car, he left me open-mouthed as he disappeared in the direction of Ibiza, tail lights twinkling, a delicate hand fluttering a farewell out of the car window.

❧

The excitement of building the first fire in my new chimney was tremendous. I knew that the damp autumn weather could make lighting it difficult but I had found in the past that the local newspaper made a good starter for the kindling, and to make sure that all went well I had two copies that were bone dry from being under my mattress and a bundle of dry twigs. Also, I'd kept two boxes of matches in my pockets during the day and under my pillow at night. This may seem a bit excessive but the reason for this was that matches in Ibiza in those days were terrible. Damp would get into the head and as you struck it on the side of the box, it would crumble, usually leaving the only spark it had produced either burning an attractive hole in your best sweater or raising a blister on your hand. The shaft of the match was rolled and waxed paper and this would collapse the second you tried to light the match. Then, more often than not the head would drop on your carpet with a similar result to your sweater. The only way of dealing with this was to use body heat to keep them dry.

I had learned how to lay a fire from my grandmother and this I now put into practice. First the newspaper was rolled corner to corner and then tied in a simple knot in the middle and the ends were tucked into the centre of the donut-shaped object. These were stacked in the hearth in a sort of cone shape. Twigs and small branches formed the kindling and were placed leaning inwards on the paper and finally some larger pieces of firewood were placed on the entire structure. The theory was that you would light around the base of the tepee-shaped cone and the rolled up paper would burn upwards with increasing heat, lighting as it went both the twigs and the firewood.

Seven o'clock arrived and so did my guests. Most of them had the same idea as Pierre and my log pile increased dramatically in size. Maria, my neighbour, had popped in with a couple of bottles and stayed to help. Corks were pulled, food was served and I realised that this was going to be a typical Ibiza party.

You'd invite, as I had, 15 people and each one would bring two or three others and what had started out as a simple drinks and something to eat affair could well go on for a couple of days with people going home for a sleep and a shower, and then coming back for Round Two. Even Pep, the farmer from up the road, tied his horse and cart to the bumper of one of the cars and came in to see what was going on. I had to explain to newcomers to the island that Pep was a relatively common name and so to avoid any confusion, logically they became Pep the Chimney and Pep the Farm.

At 10pm, the time had come for the ceremonial lighting. I handed the matches to my faithful builder and asked if he would strike the first match. "*Caray, Señor,*" he muttered. "*Es un gran honor.* I only hope it works!" Pep seemed slightly nervous and he struck the match a mighty blow against the side of the box. It fell apart in his hands showering both of us in phosphor. Pep giggled somewhat maniacally I thought. Maybe that extra *Ciento Tres* cognac hadn't been such a good idea.

It appeared that second time lucky was his motto, however, and he carefully lit the fire around the base. As it flickered and then burned, the smoke poured up the chimney with not a trace coming into the room. A spontaneous round of applause burst from everyone and as Pep stood watching, he took off his cap and scratched at his scalp as though he couldn't believe what was happening. Gradually the logs took hold and within minutes we were all clustered around the fireplace admiring the blaze. I went round with a wide variety of bottles and topped up all the glasses. "Pep," I said, "A toast to you and to the new chimney. May you always have fire in you." There was a roar of laughter as Maria laughed, "*Su mujer a dicho lo mismo.* His wife said the same."

I had a warm winter with the chimney in the sitting room and the stove burning merrily in my bedroom. The house was really dry for the first time, even though I had to shuttle back and forth to the wood yard. Finally, I arranged for the delivery of a small lorry load of logs but there were two things wrong with it. The first was that the quality of the logs was not as good as when I chose them myself and secondly, I missed the thrill of the log chase.

The following autumn, winter came early and I lit my fires in mid-September. While the days were fine, the evenings were distinctly chilly if I failed to get them going by 5pm. One misty evening I arrived home quite late with Katherine and quickly lit both fires. I left her keeping an eye on things while I went through to the kitchen to open a bottle of wine and it was while I was hunting for the corkscrew that there was an almighty crash from the sitting room. A billow of dust shot through the door and spread itself daintily over the kitchen and bathroom floors as well as the work surfaces where I was standing. A frantic coughing came from the sitting room and Katherine appeared in the kitchen doorway. Gone was the elegant person I'd arrived home with and in its place was a figure covered from head to foot in brick dust. To her enormous and ever-lasting credit she started laughing. In fact, she laughed until tears started to run down her cheeks, making slightly muddy rivulets in the dust.

"What happened," I asked anxiously as I peered through the dust-laden gloom into the sitting room.

"One minute the chimney was burning like a dream," she spluttered, "and I was just having cosy thoughts and then suddenly there was a cracking noise and the whole lot fell to the floor. Darling, do you think I could have glass of wine? My mouth is vaguely Sahara-ish."

Having cleaned and then administered a large glass of wine, I fought my way through to the site of the wreck. It was clear that the newly-lit fire hadn't survived the fall and there was no danger of anything catching fire. On the other hand, every single object was covered in inches of soot, brick and plaster dust.

There wasn't a whole lot to do and I went back to the kitchen to see how Katherine was getting on. Clearly the wine was improving her morale if not her morals.

"I wonder if I could have a bath, darling," she asked. "And could you pop my clothes in the washing machine? I can't stand here looking like a building site."

She traipsed into the bathroom and a few minutes later, a slender arm appeared round the door as she handed an assortment of delicate clothing to me. I got the washing machine going and then started to sweep the debris back in the direction of the sitting room. This took me quite a while and then I wiped down every surface in sight. Gradually all the rooms returned to normal except where the chimney had come down.

Finally the bathroom door opened and Katherine appeared swathed in a towel. She shivered delicately and said, "Darling, it's a bit chilly without any clothes and there's only one room that's warm and that's your bedroom, so I guess we'd better go in there. I must say, demolishing part of your house is a hell of a way to get a girl into bed. As Maria would say, I hope it hasn't put out *your* fire."

The following morning, I went in search of Pep. The first port of call was the nearby bar to ask Jaume if he knew where I could find my now ex-builder. "I haven't seen him for a couple of weeks, *amigo mio*. Why, do you want something else built?"

I explained what had happened and there was just the slightest hint of the corners of his mouth starting to curve upwards. "*Hombre, que mala suerte* – this is very unlucky as we are now approaching the winter. I will have to see if I can find him for you as soon as possible."

As it happened, Jaume didn't find Pep, but I did some days later. One afternoon, I dropped into a bar to meet some friends who lived near Santa Gertrudis and there, slumped in a chair next to the chimney, was my hero. Clearly lunch had been extensive and liquid and as the bar door closed, he opened his bleary eyes and quickly closed them again. Obviously word had reached him that I wanted to have a discussion about my now defunct fireplace. I went over and shook his shoulder none too gently. "*Buenos tardes, Pep, quisiero hablar con Vd*, I want to have a word with you about my chimney. Or rather, what was my chimney because as I'm sure you've heard by now, it has fallen down. I want to know why it happened."

Pep seemed to be lost in thought for a few minutes as he considered his reply. He then uttered a sentence that for sheer cheek, completely took my breath away. "*Señor,*" he responded, "it happened because last year I didn't know as much as I know this year. But I'll be happy to come and rebuild it. I could even give you a pretty good discount as this is your second chimney."

The other drinkers stopped listening and hurriedly turned away while the owner of the bar found he had something urgent to do in a back room. Nature, as they say, seemed to hold its breath and Pep appeared to realise he'd said something that might just be a tiny bit controversial. He closed his eyes, pulled his cap down firmly on his brow and retreated within himself.

To be honest, I really didn't know how to reply. Part of me wanted to say yes because I couldn't think where else I could find another builder before next Easter and part of me wanted to bean Pep with a large chunk of brick from my chimney. At that exact moment my friends arrived. They told me afterwards that it was like walking into a different dimension. Everything had frozen as though time was flowing past and not touching the occupants of the bar. Eventually I realised they were there, unglued myself from the spot on which I had become stuck and we left at high speed with me discussing Pep's ancestors and whether his mother had ever met his father more than the one time.

16.
Doves of Peace

I've always had a fear of mice and rats. It isn't logical or rational but it exists and there's nothing I can do about it. People have teased me about the dear little creatures with their tiny hands and feet, long elegant tails and whiffly little noses, but it's no good, terror strikes me when I come close to them. I've always thought that my encounters with mice actually began with a pair of doves.

Further over in my valley was a farm that I'd never visited, nor had I met the owner. But each evening a cloud of white doves would take off from the farm and circle over the fields and trees looking like elegantly folded napkins and gradually I became fixated on them. They looked so wonderful coming in to land on the roof of the farm and the occasional one would drift off course and float in my direction. The dove would land on the algarroba tree in the field in front of my house, preen itself busily for a few moments, occasionally dropping a startling-white feather that looked as though it had been laundered like a starched shirt front, then launch itself in the direction of home landing delicately some moments later on the roof of the barn next to the main house.

I was walking through the Marina one day, an area of Ibiza Town that ranged up the lower slopes of the hill towards D'Alt Vila, when I noticed something white moving in a cage at the back of the pet shop. I went in and there in front of me was a real live dove with a price tag on its cage. The owner, a small moustachioed man came out and greeted me. "*Buenos dias, Señor*, I see that you are admiring my *paloma,* my dove. It really is mine, but I cannot keep it because I am forced to live in a very small apartment here in the town and it would not be fair to keep such a beautiful creature anywhere but in the country." At this point I suppose I went mad. I was already buying a horse, I had a Labrador and a ginger tom – why not have a pair of doves as well? I agreed that the dove had to find a home in the country and I was absolutely the right person to take care of it.

"Ah, but there is a slight problem, *Señor*. You see, it would be cruel to keep *la paloma* on its own. You should only have a pair and I would be very happy to find just the right mate for this *paloma*. I believe you are exactly the right person to have such a pair of divine birds."

And, of course, I agreed with him and asked him to find me the perfect mate for this bird. "Ah, but there is one further, but small problem, *Señor*. Two birds must have a bigger cage than this but I will arrange it with a *carpintero*, a friend of mine. He will make the birds a wonderful new home." I handed over a rather larger sum of money than I had first thought and went on my way, with instructions to return in a week's time.

Seven days later I went back and was greeted by two large and rather smug doves in something that resembled the White House. My new friend congratulated me on my purchase and then dropped the bombshell. "Of course, *Señor*, you understand that these beautiful *palomas* will have to spend six months in their new home before you can let them out. They must become accustomed to their new surroundings and ideally you should keep them in your home before letting them out. I look forward to seeing you each week when you come back for more seed." In something of a daze, I loaded the doves into the back of my car and headed for home.

Over the next six months, the two birds ate prodigious quantities of seed and grew to enormous proportions and I began to fear that they would never leave the cage alive, but finally the great day came and I invited some friends around for lunch and to watch the launch of my aerial circus. Once we were all feeling vaguely soporific, I dragged the box out onto the terrace aided by one or two sniggering friends, opened the cage door and went back to my chair. My two overweight, not to say fat avian companions peered nervously at the exit to the East Wing of the White House. They resembled the guest who came to dinner and stayed for six months. I placed a handful of succulent seed in front of their door and gradually they edged towards the exit from their home. Finally one of them placed a nervous claw on the edge of the doorway as though he had heard he could fly but wasn't convinced by the rumour. He (or she – I never could tell) wriggled through the door and with a tremendous leap of faith, headed for the sky.

Having watched the first dove with some care, the second one shot through the door like a feathery cannon ball from the barrel of the gun and together they flew onto my roof. We all regarded them with awe. The sniggerers stopped their unseemly noise and one or two people congratulated me. They exclaimed that I had managed the impossible and, after six months in a health spa, the birds had proved their worth. The terrible two sitting on the roof regarded us with expressions of horror as we tried to tempt them back to their home as I crept up onto the roof with handfuls of seed that I scattered at their feet. They gave me a distinctly old-fashioned look, glanced at each other like a pair of elderly Duchesses who had confirmed that my breeding wasn't up to scratch and took off. They circled once until they'd found their bearings and then headed straight back to the Marina district of Ibiza town. The following week, as I passed the pet shop, I spied a pair of grossly overweight doves in a cage at the back of the shop. Whether they were mine, who can say but by then I had lost interest in the dreadful duo.

The small wood-burning stove in my bedroom figured heavily in the problem of my fear of mice. The stove had a metal chimney that ran up the corner of my bedroom and through the roof and soon after my feathered friends had made their break for freedom, a mouse obviously found some of the seed I'd left on the roof in a vain attempt to bribe them to stay. I was asleep at about 3am on a hot summer's night when I was woken by a strange whiffling, falling, flumping noise. There was no one else in the house and it was only after a certain amount of research that I opened the door to the stove. Obviously it hadn't burned for a while, but there was a layer of ash at the bottom and, to my horror, a small mouse was peering blearily back out at me. I shut the door hurriedly and considered my options. One thing was clear. I wouldn't spend the night alone in the same bedroom as a mouse, so wearily I collected hammer and cold chisel, freed the metal chimney from its concrete collar in the ceiling and dragged the stove out onto the terrace. There, I opened the door and retreated.

The mouse examined the outside world for a moment, hopped onto what one might call the porch of the stove and then legged it straight back into the house because I had forgotten to shut the front door. With a cry of despair, I followed the wretched creature as it shot into the kitchen and into a cupboard. I managed to wedge the door shut and once again, I thought about my options. In the end, I shut the kitchen door, retreated to my bedroom and slept the sleep of the mouse-less just.

The following morning, I could hear a rustling noise from the cupboard. Obviously, my houseguest was up and about and expecting breakfast and the only way I could help both him and me was by evicting him from the house.

I went out to my local *carpinteria*, the carpenter's workshop, bought sheets of hardboard and lengths of battening and returned home. Having nailed the sheets to the battening until I had a mouse run which could be attached to the cupboard and eventually led to my back door, I collected a beer, a book and a chair and settled down outside the backdoor. Eventually a somewhat overfed mouse emerged from my mouse run and tottered off into the late afternoon sunshine. I found that the cupboard had contained a packet of biscuits that were obviously part of a mouse diet. I hurried up to the roof, swept it clear of any trace of bird seed and replaced the stove in the bedroom. Once again my home was rodent free. But my car wasn't.

I'd only just bought a Renault 4. This extraordinary vehicle was like a flat bed truck that you could drive over the worst surfaces, fill with vast quantities of junk, occasionally feed with a small amount of fuel and never a word of complaint would you hear. The Citroen Dyane was exactly the same but I always felt the Renault 4 had the edge in terms of strength and reliability.

I had two versions of the same car. The first one I bought second-hand soon after I arrived on the island, and to be honest, it wasn't in the best of shape. It had a strange, distinctly offensive smell of damp and I assumed it came from the previous owner having carried something… well, wet… and that it would fade away. I suspect that the former driver kept the windows open for a week before he sold it to me. It was a horrible, tomb-like odour that was only made worse by putting on the heating in a vain attempt to dry out the car.

Friends used to climb in and as they settled in the seats, you could see the smell hit them somewhere between the eyes. They'd look wildly round trying to identify the source and then you'd notice a surreptitious hand come up and even on the coldest and wettest days, the hand would open the window. Invariably there'd be a, "Good heavens, what a warm day," or, "Bit stuffy in here," remark and they'd lean heavily towards the open air where they'd appear to be doing deep-breathing exercises. Even my Labrador, who normally enjoyed anything he could find that was disgusting and decayed, used to resist any blandishments to get him into the car. Certainly, there was nothing wrong with the bodywork that I could see and since the car lived out of doors and I acquired it in late summer, the smell wasn't really making its presence felt too strongly at that point.

September came and with it the first autumn rains. Gradually the *caminos* lost the hard surface they'd acquired with the sun beating down on them and where there were holes, these filled with water and mud. It was now that I discovered where the strange aroma came from. After a really heavy downpour I was driving along the unsealed road into Ibiza as it wound past what is now the Roca Llisa golf course. There was a particularly deep crater into which the front end of the car dipped with all the enthusiasm of a dolphin. As it started to rise up the other side, a jet of freezing cold water shot in through the floor where the pedals were located and disappeared up my right trouser where it nestled somewhere around my right knee.

I braked abruptly and the water that had entered and fallen on the floor leapt happily into my *espadrille*. These, as you probably know, have a material upper and a rope sole so getting them wet means they stay that way for some time. On the other hand, they were the only shoes I had with me so I ploughed on, feeling less than charitable about the man who'd sold me the car. By this time, I could swear pretty fluently in both Spanish and English and I made the most of this new skill. The smell of damp returned with a vengeance and it wasn't long before I phoned the garage in Ibiza town.

I took the car in and tried to persuade the service department to weld a sheet of metal over the hole, just leaving the pedals sticking through. In their turn they managed to persuade me that my car was ready to go to the great repair shop in the sky and that I should consider replacing it with something newer.

"After all," explained Alfredo, the manager of the showroom who was massaging my right arm soothingly as we strolled among the various vehicles parked neatly alongside one another, "*Los coches*, the cars are like the humans. As you have found with your present car and the, what we might call air-conditioning in the floor, they get old, things start to go wrong and although you are young now, *Señor*, one day, please God, you will be old and you will understand what I mean." Clasping my arm in a firm grip, he led me over to a brand new car. "Why not sit in the new version that we have here. It is so *confortable*, so smooth running," and here he paused for a second while he considered how to word his masterstroke. He coughed delicately like a major domo announcing the arrival of the honoured guest. "It is so, so, *seco*, so dry inside. There are no, ahem, no holes in the floor and your *espadrillos* will stay very comfortable."

At this point his hand left my arm for a second, just long enough to open the door and to usher me inside with enormous deference, the major domo once again playing a starring role. "Feel how the seat is so firm and yet soft, note how you can adjust it to accommodate your distance from the pedals; perhaps you would like to take *el coche* for a drive around the streets? Look, I will come with you so that you will not get lost," and with that he slipped into the passenger seat with the alacrity and smoothness of a boa constrictor that has spied lunch. Within seconds, I found myself turning the key in the ignition and I was driving out of the showroom.

Suddenly I realised just how the gears on my old car had been sticking as I changed down (I had already started to think of it in the past tense). There had been that unpleasant grating, ripping noise sometimes as I tried to put it into reverse and from time to time I was aware of the front suspension lacking a certain ability to bounce back when I went over a hump in the road. Add to that the occasional need to ask passers-by to help me bump start the car or to park on a hill so that I could give the poor old thing a shove and then run round to the driver's door, throw myself in, slam down the clutch and then let it up with a jolt while saying a prayer to the engine gods that it would catch, and you could say I was ripe for the plucking. To be honest, I was quite fed up with visiting friends and, as I left, having to ask the more muscular members of the company if they could give me a shove. I'd noticed a few of them giving me a dirty look sometimes and I realised that the time had come to say goodbye.

I tried suggesting that the garage might give me something for my old car but Alfredo's feelings on the subject were summed up in the way he looked at me. I got the impression that if I pursued the subject, he might have asked me to contribute to its burial fund. I'd always been fairly anthropomorphic about inanimate objects. I tended to treat them as old friends and, crazy as it may sound, I felt guilty if I got rid of them. And part of me had just the same feeling about the old car. It had done its best and I was grateful, but I did like the feeling of security, of everything working, of plain newness about the model I was driving and as we arrived back at the showroom, Alfredo asked, "*Que le parece? Esta bien, no?* It feels good, doesn't it?" He'd assessed my mood perfectly, seen the look on my face and he went on, "Don't bother driving it inside, it'll be absolutely safe outside while we do the paperwork."

These days, the process of buying a car involves sheet after sheet of forms, signature after signature, the organisation of the finance, the sorting out of the road tax, the insurance, the breakdown service, even the code for the radio so that should the battery ever be disconnected, you'd know how to re-programme it.

Life was simpler in those days. Then it was just a question of organising the money by strolling around the corner to the Vara de Rey, popping into your bank, drawing out the appropriate amount (always assuming you, and the bank, had enough) and possibly stopping and having a San Miguel in a bar just to keep you going. You'd then drop into your insurance company's office, tell them the good news that they'd have to insure your new car, wait while they drew up the policy, compare notes on what they drove, have your back slapped in congratulation on having made such a sensible decision, stroll back to the showroom via the *Correos*, the Post Office, check your *apartado*, your mail box which would invariably be empty, and then go and hand over the cash. There would be a couple of forms to fill in, your licence had to be produced plus proof of insurance and you were done. There were no call centres to irritate you, no asking you for the same information 84 times 'for security purposes'. Everything was done at a controlled and gentle pace.

The chances were that you'd be invited to pop around the corner and celebrate your purchase with the head of the garage. This might, if the timing was right, turn into a lunch of half a dozen *tapas* and a bottle of wine and then, before you knew it, you were inhaling the smell that all brand new cars have, turning the key and slipping it silkily into gear as you drove off with the open road ahead of you. I was so pleased with my new car that I visited several friends that afternoon just to prove that they no longer had to bump start my car.

I realised as I drove along that the main difference between it and my recently retired old friend was that everything worked. The same, very odd gear stick that was mounted high up on the dashboard and connected with the gear box at the front of the engine that was common to the Citroen Mehari, the Deux Chevaux, the Renault 4 and the Dyane, the same windows that slid back and forwards rather than up and down and while the controls, dials and interior fittings were definitely primitive, it had a huge plus in its favour. It knew all about starting with the turn of a key.

And, of course, with the way the rear seats folded down, it was like having a small, flat bed truck. It was entirely practical and it wasn't long before I was using it to its full extent. With the onset of the colder weather, I went back to buying my logs from the log yard. Up with the back door of the car, baskets of logs emptied inside and I was away home with another load of instant heating. Somehow, carrying around large quantities of logs never seemed that much of a task when they smelled as delicious as almond, algarroba or pine logs do. And there's that wonderful moment when the weather is cold enough to light the first fire of the winter, that moment when the warmth spreads throughout the rooms. It's different from central heating. It's a bone-warming, damp-drying, soothing kind of heat that makes life feel infinitely better. And when you've a flat-topped, cast-iron stove in your bedroom of the kind that you see in Western movies, there's a perfect excuse for putting the ingredients of a hot toddy or mulled wine in a saucepan and placing it on the stove. The smell spreads gradually through the house and you notice people relaxing.

I'd learned the way to make mulled wine many years before and for me, it's the best, heart-warming winter drink. All you need is the cheapest red wine, white sugar, diced oranges and lemons, cloves, a cinnamon stick and a large slurp of brandy (if you have it to hand); it's quick, easy and cheap to make – and tastes wonderful!

What wasn't quite so great was the fact that I realised someone was living in my new car. I realised I had an additional passenger when I found well-chewed bits of foam on the front seat as well as scrunched up shreds of wood bark. Having dismissed the idea of geckos and lizards, I couldn't imagine what it was but I rather hoped it would stop before the front seat was demolished. Despite keeping an eagle eye open, I couldn't figure it out.

The Renault 4 had a bench-like front seat and it wasn't until I was driving into Santa Eulalia one day that I just happened to glance in the mirror. There, to my horror, staring back at me was a small mouse who'd been tiptoeing along the back of the front seat. He (or she – hard to tell really and I didn't stop to ask) looked for all the world like Jerry out of the Tom and Jerry cartoon. Our eyes met for a millisecond and with a startled leap, he disappeared into the back of the car.

Screeching to a halt at the side of the road and, feeling like the heroine of a Victorian novel who spies a mouse and leaps onto a chair yelling, "Eeek," I tumbled out of the car as fast as I could. Flinging all the doors open, I searched high and low for the wretched rodent but my miniature Houdini had done a runner. I waited 15 minutes but the villain of the piece had vanished totally. It was too much to hope that he'd shot out of the open window so I climbed cautiously back in the car, turned it round and headed home at high speed. I parked outside the house and went in to collect my secret weapon.

Some time before I'd been walking past the same pet shop in which I'd bought the doves. Though my feelings towards the shop and its keeper had been hardened by the doves' treachery, there was no way I could resist what I saw. Lying at the back of a cage in the window was a Siamese kitten with the most startlingly blue eyes and fur like a miniature seal. Despite the heat of the afternoon, she came bounding up to the glass and peered back up at me. Where her nose pressed against the window, there was a small damp circle and I bent down to look at her. I went in and 15 minutes later emerged with the kitten that I christened Shakira. As she grew up she never learned to yowl like Siamese cats are supposed to do, which was definitely a relief. Rather, she'd let out a strange little 'ehh' sound if, for example, she wanted the front door opened or milk in her bowl. What she did learn was to travel round the living room without once touching the ground. Chair backs, curtains and shelves were all one to her and on a good day nothing was knocked off and nothing torn. On a bad day, everything would go flying and any fabrics in her path were in danger of having chunks torn off them.

Of course, for anyone who knows anything about Siamese cats, this is the way they prefer to travel. The ground is, quite literally, beneath them. According to a breeder I once talked to, there's a legend that Siamese cats would go into battle sitting on their owner's shoulders and then leap on the enemy. Whether this accounts for their ability to climb, or not, I don't know. What I do know is that this scrap of fur grew into one of the most beautiful creatures I'd ever seen and while Tanit, my ginger tom, would tolerate affection on his own terms, Shakira craved it.

And she would repay all the stroking, scratching and tickling as well. In some strange way, she could sense when someone had, for example, a pain in their arm or their hip or a headache. You'd see her deliberately climb onto their lap or wherever the pain was located and she'd wrap herself around the afflicted part and then go into a deep sleep. Whether she actually knew she was helping or whether it was just an animal instinct, I can definitely remember having bad headaches when she'd climb onto my shoulder, curl up round my neck and stay there quite quietly. On the other hand, Shakira was a demon at chasing lizards. However agile and however fast they were, she was that much faster and I had high hopes that mice might well be to her taste.

After my Encounter at Mouse Car-ral, I explained carefully to her that I had an important mission for her and that she'd have to spend the night in the car. Carrying her out to the Renault, I examined the interior but there was no sign of its occupant. I carefully opened the door, slipped Shakira and a bowl of water but no food into the car and left, closing the door carefully behind me. As I went back into the house, I thought that if there was any way of catching the mouse, it had to be my Siamese.

The following morning, I woke up feeling quite cheerful. I remembered my neat solution to the mouse problem and lay in bed hoping that its end had been swift, that Shakira had been efficient at despatching it and that the mess I'd have to deal with wouldn't be too bad. By the time I'd showered, I wondered what little treat I could buy Shakira to thank her.

I went out to the car and crept up to the driver's window. What I saw filled me with horror for there, lying on the front seat was my over-fed traitor of a cat snoring quietly while the mouse, clearly feeling no pain, was relaxing in the sun that shone on the top of the front passenger seat. "Faithless hussy," I hissed at my sinful Siamese through the closed window. "How could you do it? Why didn't you rend the wretched rodent in two? What do you mean by lying there like a drunk sleeping off the night before?"

Shakira opened her eyes sleepily, peered round her as though she was surprised at her surroundings and stretched luxuriously. Clearly she'd enjoyed her night in the car but now she was more alert and she suddenly saw the mouse. At exactly the same moment the mouse did a somersault and fell onto the floor in the front. Without waiting to let the situation develop any further, he disappeared.

But now I'd spotted where he was living. The Renault 4 bench front seat was mounted on a transverse metal box and I'd noticed my tenant disappear into an arch-like hole cut into the front. Clearly he'd set up home in somewhat palatial circumstances and, of course, living in the country, I realised my shoes probably brought in a selection of seeds and grasses while bark from the logs I brought home probably acted a kind of larder. I never did figure out what the creature did for water but doubtless I would have provided enough in the winter when I got in with wet shoes.

This was all very cosy but it couldn't go on. I began to feel like one of those characters in chase scenes in the movies as I drove along. I found myself driving faster and staring over my shoulder with a hunted stare in case there was any wildlife peering back at me over my shoulder.

I decided that either the car would have to go or its occupant. However, the decision was rather taken out of my hands some two or three weeks later. I'd parked the car in Ibiza Town, locked it up and gone off to meet some friends. Over lunch I explained my predicament to Karl, a German who lived near Santa Eulalia and who I'd done some translation for. Having described the episode of the mouse creeping along the back of the seat in graphic detail, I was surprised at his lack of sympathy when he practically collapsed with laughter. Tears ran down his face as he beckoned over Jan, a Dutch friend of his. They nearly had hysterics when I described Shakira snoozing quietly on the front seat with the mouse nearby and Karl immediately called for another bottle of white wine.

"Stewart, *mein freund*, this is *wunderbar*. Ze maus living in ze auto is too much. It is like a child's comic. Maybe ve could sell ze idea to a TV company. We will find a solution but first we must drink to the health of your cat who loves mouses zo much." And rather reluctantly I clinked glasses with the two of them to toast Shakira.

In point of fact, the solution was rather simpler than I thought.

I had gone to the airport one evening in an absolute downpour to pick up Jim, a neighbour of mine who was coming back from the frozen north, well, East Anglia, on the last flight of the day. I left my car in the car park on a sort of corner that seemed alright to me and ran to the terminal building. There was the usual degree of chaos as the travellers came through passport control and friends and families walked straight through Customs to greet them with hugs and kisses and to talk about how the journey had been, how the relatives were, had they enjoyed the trip to Paris, London or one of many other places.

Gradually everybody sorted themselves out with the correct bags and headed outside. By the time we emerged the rain had stopped and between us we carried his luggage out to the car. I had the back door open and we were just about to put his suitcases in the boot when I spotted my small furry passenger legging it for home under the front seat. "Bloody hell," I moaned, "this is quite ridiculous. My life's become a misery since you went away."

Jim looked startled and then laughed. "I didn't know you cared," he giggled happily.

"No, it's not that, I'm absolutely fed up with being terrified to get in my own car."

"What are you scared of?" he asked interestedly.

"Why, that blasted four legged pest, that wretched mouse that's taken up residence in what was once, upon a very short time ago, a nice new vehicle. You remember the trouble I had with the one that fell into my stove last summer and then got into a kitchen cupboard? I can't stand the blasted things. I feel like putting a bomb under the car."

"Oh yes, I do recall your reaction to having a house guest. It was the talk of all the neighbours. Jonno, that Australian off the oil rigs who spent the summer in Santa Eulalia went around telling everyone about it. But you've two cats," he went on, "why can't you get them to deal with it?"

"I've tried," I bleated in irritation. "Tanit's too old and Shakira was completely useless. I found her snuggled up against the horrible creature after she'd spent the night in the car."

"Well, show me where the mouse is living. I'm pretty sure I can think of at least two possible solutions," he went on.

I opened the driver's door while he went round to the passenger's side. "Lean down," I said. "You see that hole in the metal that's supporting the seat. The monster goes in and out of there as cool as you please as though he owns the place."

"And you can't remove the seat and get at it in any other way?

"No, I've even been under the car to see if there's hole there but the answer's still no."

"Well, in that case the first answer's pretty obvious. Put some food inside the hole and wait to make sure the mouse is in there and then slide some poison in as well. Block the hole up and the chances are that your car guest will have become the late unlamented."

"But that's terrible. I'd be driving around sitting on top of its corpse. Besides, I may hate the thing, but I don't like to think of it having a slow, lingering death. And imagine the smell."

"Lord, you do make things difficult. Well, look the second solution may be more to your taste. While I was back in the UK

I took my driving test so now I can drive here. I'm going to have to buy a car anyway and apart from having a tenant, this one is virtually brand new. I don't mind mice at all, so why don't I buy the car from you, with a small adjustment in the price of course, as it's not completely new and it's had two owners, one quite a lot smaller than the other. If you're agreeable, of course."

I thought about it for a moment. Needless to say there'd be all the paperwork to complete at some cost and I knew this would add to the stories about how strange I was when it came to mice, but I couldn't go on having to catch the bus because the thought of having the creature playing tag along the top of the back seat gave me the shivers. There'd be the explanations when I went to buy yet another Renault and I could imagine the ripple of delighted laughter that would ring around the car showroom, but it would all be worth it.

"Do you really mean it?" I asked.

"Well, it seems to be the kindest solution for all three of us! Clearly you're feeling trapped," he laughed, delighted with his joke.

"Oh get in and let's go home and have drink."

A couple of days later, we completed the transaction and the only thing that remained for me to do was to go into Ibiza and see if the garage had a new car in stock. Jim offered to drive me in for which I was grateful. As I walked over to his house, I saw my old vehicle parked outside. There seemed to be a notice of some sort taped on the inside of the rear window. As I got closer, I could see what it said. In large capitals, Jim had written:

"Jim's New Mickey Mousemobile"

17.
The Long March Home

A month later, I found myself on a bus heading back to the Costa del Sol and Adelfa. It was a night bus and seriously over-crowded. Managing to find an aisle seat was a bonus, and as the bus swung out of Alicante bus station, I settled down to sleep. As national transport services go, this wasn't exactly like the US Greyhound buses. The seats had definitely been through several former incarnations and the springs were doing their best to break free. Also, the amount of leg room was minimal. But it also had its charms, such as stopping every half an hour or so at different bars along the way. At one point during the night, I was dozing in my seat with my arm hanging down when I was woken by a large and obviously male hand gently stroking mine. I quickly withdrew it, waking the Spaniard in the seat on the other side of the aisle. Embarrassment covered his face as he realised what he had done and he apologised profusely. "*Señor*, I am so sorry. Believe me, I am truly sorry. But you see, I was dreaming of my girl friend and when I felt your arm I thought it was her."

The next time the bus stopped, he insisted on buying me half a tumbler of cognac and a *bocadillo de jamon*, ham in an enormous and extremely hard roll, as a further apology. He was obviously well known and by now we were beginning to see the funny side of things. He told the barman what had happened and within seconds the story had been repeated and repeated until it seemed as though everyone in the neighbourhood knew what had happened. By the time we climbed aboard the bus once more a small crowd had gathered to cheer us on. Then, of course, everyone on the bus had to be told the story until my new friend had tears of laughter running down his cheeks and the bus was in an uproar. Some of the passengers had bottles of wine in their luggage and these were quickly opened and shared around.

Finally we arrived in Malaga and from there I took a rattling old taxi all the way to Fifi and Rafael's *cortijo*. On arrival I found tremendous excitement as they practised loading and unloading little Adelfa into her brand new travelling box. That night was spent on the farm and after a wonderful dinner I wandered out to the stables to nuzzle and scratch Adelfa's soft muzzle. I was greeted by those deep-in-the-throat mutters that horses give when they are happy and I went back to my bedroom overjoyed in the knowledge that I'd made the right decision.

The following morning, Adelfa was led into her box and the back panel was bolted securely onto the sides. The whole thing was then pushed up a ramp and onto a waiting truck. Three bales of hay and three of straw were loaded behind her box and a drum of drinking water for me and off we set for the nearest railway station. At this point I began to feel very nervous. Up to this moment, it had all seemed so easy. I guessed my little horse had wandered into her travelling box so happily because she knew she could wander out when she wanted to. But when the back panel was put on I had caught a look of utter astonishment in her eyes. And as the box was pushed onto the lorry, her ears went back for a moment and the imperiousness that many generations of breeding had given her showed as she stamped one delicate hoof.

The railway workers took one look at her and there were a great many "*hombres*" and "*que caballo*" as Adelfa and I entered the wagon that was to be our home for the next 16 hours – or so we thought. If I say that the next few days were some of the worst I've ever experienced, it's no exaggeration.

The problems started about eight hours after we left the station. Adelfa, having dozed for quite a while, suddenly found that the whole concept of rail travel didn't suit her and she decided to kick her way out of her travelling box. The back started to disintegrate quickly, and then she began to try and rear up. My first worry was for her, the fear she was obviously feeling and how near she was to harming herself. The second thought was for my bank manager who wouldn't be too happy if anything happened to her and how he might start rearing and kicking out as well.

Thankfully, I'd loaded some lengths of rope into the wagon at the last minute and I used these to cross tie her so that she couldn't rear. Then I poured some of my drum of water over Adelfa as I fought to calm her. By now we were approaching a station, and I leant out of the wagon and yelled at people on the platform, "Get a vet, *necesito un veterinario*, I have a horse here that must have a *calmante, un tranquilizante*." The train was moving slowly by now but clearly wasn't going to stop. Thankfully, however, one of the workers shouted back, "I'll make sure there's a vet waiting at the next station, *no te preocupes*." All my fears now surged to the fore as I tried to imagine how I was going to cope with such a highly volatile horse. Needless to say, I was highly *preocupado* because I didn't know how far away the next station was.

Thankfully, I also didn't know at that point just how far and wide across Spain I'd range with my little Arab mare. It turned out I was on a slow goods train that ran up to Cordoba and then further north in the direction of Madrid. I had to leave Adelfa in the care of a couple of railway workers in Cordoba as I took a taxi to a laboratory that specialised in veterinary products. There they made up a bottle of tranquilliser that could be added to water without clashing with whatever injections a vet might give her. It's certainly an unusual way to gain your first glimpse of a city, shuttling frantically from station to outskirts to station again in the back of a taxi owned by an excessively cheerful driver. Years later I went back to the city and discovered how beautiful it really is, but on that occasion I had no time to enjoy anything.

Time passed and it was then that I found out just how kind the Spanish can be to a stranger in distress, especially one with a horse. Somehow I managed to find vets who helped me to keep Adelfa calm with sedatives and gradually we started to turn east. After passing through small towns, constantly filling my barrel of water at stations where the train stopped to load or unload various goods and which I shared with my four legged companion, and somehow finding bales of hay and alfalfa, we gradually pulled in through the outskirts of Alicante. I had never eaten so many dried-up old rolls filled with soap-like cheese in my life as I did in those days and I longed for the chance to sit down at a bar and have a beer. But Adelfa couldn't be left and our odyssey was beginning to get me down.

Early one morning, with a squealing of brakes the train screeched to a halt a couple of hundred yards from the main Alicante station. The crew dismounted from the engine and waved farewell to me as they started to pick their way across the rails in the direction of the platforms. "*Oiga*," I yelled, "*a donde vas?* Where are you going? What about us?"

With a shrug of his shoulders, the driver called back, "*No se. Vd. va a Ibiza, non?* You're heading for Ibiza?" I shouted back in agreement and he shook his head. "You're in the wrong station – you want the one at the port."

"What do I do now?" I called, my heart sinking at the thought of yet more problems.

"You'll have to go to the office of the *jefe*, manager, of the station. It's on the platform over there." And with that, he turned and set off again.

As far as I could see, I had two choices. Either I stayed with Adelfa and hoped against hope that someone would walk past who could help. Certainly it didn't seem the kind of place where people just popped by. The other alternative was to trust to heaven that she would be all right while I went off to try and find the *jefe*. The second choice seemed the most logical and so I gave her the remains of my water and some of the last of the alfalfa and closing the door to the wagon, set off in the searing heat.

I tried stepping from one wooden sleeper to the next but I slipped off them and so tripping and stumbling over the stones between the rails, I arrived at the platform. There was a sign indicating the station director's office and standing outside guarding the door stood a stern looking *Guardia Civil*. Panting, I went up to him and started to explain my predicament. I finished by saying, "And so I must see the *jefe* to arrange to move my wagon to the port." I'd noticed that when I first walked up to him, the *Guardia Civil* had taken a couple of steps back and raised his rifle protectively across his chest. He looked at me as though I had appeared from a space ship and had horns sticking out of my head. What I hadn't realised was just how appalling I smelled and looked. I'd been living in a wagon with a horse for a few days, it was iron-hot as only mid-summer Spain can become and I hadn't washed, shaved or brushed my teeth in all that time.

When I set off on the journey with Adelfa, I'd assumed that in a few hours I'd be in Alicante. The last thing I'd thought I would need to do would be to impress my predicament on a suspicious policeman and the head of one of Spain's main railway stations. Fortunately, something in my tone must have got through the *Guardia's* outer shell. With a slightly furtive gesture, he indicated I could go in. He followed close behind me and once inside, he pointed to where I should wait while he whispered my problem to someone who looked like a male secretary. Heavy furniture, dark marble and high dusty windows made the office looked as though it hadn't changed since the day it was built and I could see motes of dust floating around in the beams of light that penetrated the dark interior of the room.

The secretary nodded and went over to a man seated behind the desk. He bent down and whispered into the man's ear. In turn he looked up at me and seemed to wince. "Do you speak

Spanish?" he asked. "If so, tell me about this horse of yours." It was at this point that I found out just how much Spanish I could now speak. I described Adelfa, who had owned her, the journey we'd undergone and how desperately I wanted to get to the port with her. I apologised for my appearance, explained how tired I was and that the only sleep I'd had was sitting on a bale of alfalfa and leaning against the wall of the wagon

"*Tambien me encanta los caballos,* I too love horses," he smiled, "but I prefer the *Andaluz* breed. I appreciate their size and strength. However, we must see what we can do to help you." He beckoned his secretary who bent down once more. The *jefe* muttered at some length and then turned back to me. "I have given orders that your wagon will be moved at once to the port where it will be cooler anyway. Also, my secretary will contact the ferry company and ensure that you can travel today. In addition, you will be given water and food for your horse."

I moved to shake his hand and to thank him, but he swayed back in his seat as the *Guardia* started to reach out to grab me but obviously he too thought better of it. Clearly my aura travelled before me. "It is nothing. Just make sure you have a bath the next time you come to Alicante Station," laughed the *jefe*. "I envy you your horse very much, *Señor* but not the journey you have made." Once again I set off along the tracks in the direction of my wagon. By now the heat was unbearable and opening the wagon door, I saw that Adelfa was drooping like a wilting flower.

Within minutes, a strange little engine came chugging along towards us. The railwaymen uncoupled our wagon from the previous train, hooked it up behind the engine and once more we were on our way. It was a brief journey and before long we were on the quayside. Here the sea breeze cooled the wagon and my little horse's head gradually lifted as she began to take interest in her surroundings. Obviously the *jefe's* message had worked because we were swiftly loaded onto a cargo ship and a bucket of fresh water was provided for Adelfa.

I checked with a crew member that the ship was heading for Ibiza. "*Si Señor*, but first we go to Palma de Mallorca. Please don't worry, you are safe now. We will make sure your horse is in a good place on the ship for the journey and we will help to look after her." Adelfa had attracted the attention of a number of sailors and as they crowded round to peer at her, I realised how much damage she had done to her travelling box. I mentioned it to one of the sailors and he agreed that it needed attention. "We don't want her to escape when we are at sea," he agreed. "I will arrange it while you go and meet *El Capitan*. He has asked that you should go up to the bridge."

One of the crew showed me the way up a number of companionways and along passages until I arrived at a door that led onto the bridge. A small and incredibly smart man came out. "*Señor* Andersen?" he murmured politely. "Er *si*, I am," I replied, once again aware of just how disgusting I must look and smell.

"Might I suggest that you come to my cabin, take a shower and we will provide you with some clean clothes, a uniform shirt and trousers. Then how would a cold glass of white wine sound? Oh, my name us Luis Ferrer. Please call me Luis."

I nearly passed out, whether from tiredness, the extraordinary kindness or the thought of the wine I don't really know. "I am so grateful. You really are kind. But first I must make sure my horse is OK."

"Please don't worry. I have a number of horse lovers among my crew and the chance to look after an Arabian mare doesn't happen every day. They will make sure she is well looked after." And with that he led me to his cabin, showed me where everything was and left me to the utter luxury of a shower, a bottle of shampoo, a razor and clean clothes. I think I must have used every last drop of hot water on the ship but finally I was clean, dressed and rather more human than I had been for some time.

I found the Captain leaning on the wing of the bridge, looking out at the city. Turning, he laughed quietly and said, "First the wine and then I would be grateful if you would introduce me to your horse. I have seen her from up here and she has the look of *una yegua de leyenda*, like a legendary horse."

He produced a bottle from inside the bridge and one of the crew brought chairs. We sat down and he poured a glass of wine that tasted like pure chilled gold. I didn't care if it cost seven pesetas a litre or if it had a plastic cap to the bottle, it was fabulous. Eventually, clutching a second large glass of wine, I followed him down the companionways until we came to the deck that led us to Adelfa.

She must have had the most forgiving nature of any horse in Spain. As we approached her box her head came up from the hand of one of the crew who had cut up an apple and was feeding it to her slice by slice. She looked at me for a moment, then shook her head as though to rearrange her hair-do and let out a gentle whinny. I reached out to her and stroked her muzzle and she pressed her head against my hand. It was only then that I realised just how badly she had scraped her muzzle and her mouth but clearly the sea air was reviving her and the after-effects of the tranquilisers must have been wearing off. The Captain now reached in to tickle and scratch her under her dark grey mane and she turned her enormous limpid eyes in his direction. For a moment, he removed his hand and she quickly pressed herself against his arm.

"*Dios mio*," he laughed, "she is like all women – such a flirt."

18.
Back Home in Ibiza

The voyage to Palma and then on to Ibiza soothed my jangled nerves, the crew found me a comfortable chair that I placed near Adelfa's box, dinner was served on a tray and suddenly it seemed as though the trials of the journey had finally ended. They had somehow threaded a narrow but strong chain through the rings in her bridle and attached these to a stanchion on either side of her. This meant that unless she could remove her head collar, she couldn't rear up or escape. And so we passed the journey to Mallorca. In Palma, the ship's agent had even managed to find some alfalfa for Adelfa who stamped rather prettily in her box with sheer excitement. Her mood seemed to have improved by leaps and bounds and her condition was obviously improving. Clearly she was a real sea horse.

Hours later and with a sigh of enormous relief, I finally saw the lights of Ibiza's picturesque port. It was just after midnight as we rounded the *muelle,* the jetty and tied up stern on to the quay. Most of the cargo was unloaded before it was our turn and it gave me time to try and spot the truck that I had booked from on board the boat during the crossing to Palma. Needless to say, it hadn't turned up and my heart sank. Eventually it was our turn to be brought off the ship and Adelfa's box was deposited carefully on the quayside. Given the lack of transport, I couldn't think of any other solution but to walk my horse the 15 kilometres home.

The nightlife in the bars on the port was in full swing and as I opened the end of the travelling box, some tourists who were rather the worse for wear spotted that something odd was going on and they came over, ever-present cameras at the ready. As Adelfa stepped daintily out and peered around, they raised their cameras and started taking pictures. She took one look at the battery of flashes and decided that she'd finally had enough. Thankfully I had a firm grip on her reins but even so I found myself being dragged along the road towards the end of the harbour. Fortunately a couple of the crew had stayed with me and they set off in hot pursuit of us. One grabbed hold of a handful of mane and the other lunged for her head collar on the opposite side to me and gradually we all skidded to a halt.

"*Señor*," the one nearest to me panted, "*hay que llamar al veterinario*, you must call the vet and get help for the horse. This is too dangerous."

I totally agreed with him and fortunately, as there was a telephone box a few yards away, I asked the crew-members if they would mind guarding her while I tried to find whether one of the island's vets was home or not. My usual one was obviously out on a call but I managed to get hold of another one. He answered the phone on the third ring and when I explained the problem, he eventually agreed to come although he sounded extremely dubious. "Are you sure, *Señor* that you really need me? It is, after all, really late." I pointed out that I had a panicky horse who needed urgent attention and could he please come as soon as possible.

I hung up and returned to my two nervous companions and Adelfa. The sailors agreed to wait with me and about 20 minutes later, the vet came sidling down the port. "*Buenas noches, Señor*, it is a very fine horse you have, but very big." I pointed out that she only stood at about 14 hands but he still looked apprehensive. Adelfa skipped sideways as a passing car hooted at us and the vet in his turn gave a sort of sideways sashay. "She is very nervous horse, *Señor*. I should be giving her tranquiliser." I agreed and he quickly unpacked an enormous syringe, filled it with a clear liquid and practically threw it at Adelfa. She seemed not to notice as he pushed the plunger home, withdrew the syringe, packed his equipment and with a brisk, "Pay me the next time we see each other," he disappeared into the night.

The two sailors explained that they had to return to their ship and I found myself on my own at the beginning of the road to Santa Eulalia with a much calmer horse and 15 kilometres to walk before we arrived at our destination. But now I was on my home turf, it was a clear, starlit night and we could take our time. I felt that the dramas of the last few days were behind me. The late night traffic had thinned out and soon after we passed a warehouse where *algarrobas*, carob beans, were stored on the left and the petrol station on the right, we turned off in the direction of the village of Jesus. Another 15 minutes saw us starting up the hill in the direction of home. The road was clear, the moon was bright and the night had that delicious warmth that you get after a really hot day. I was relaxed as we traipsed along, Adelfa not exactly picking up her feet but still keeping up with me.

Suddenly I heard a sort of grunt from her and turning, I saw her weaving like a drunk on a Saturday night. With a sigh, she collapsed in the middle of the road. "Dear Lord," I thought, "are you sure? This can't be happening. Now what do I do?"

I crouched down by her head and found that at least she was still breathing. On the other hand, I didn't know when some drunk who was out late would hurtle round the corner in his car on his way home. Gradually I managed to coax her up onto her feet and we stood there for a few minutes. After a time, we set off once more and we'd gone no more than a hundred yards when she toppled onto her side and slid backwards into a deep ditch at the side of the road. All I could see were her hooves sticking up.

I can't say I panicked because I think I was beyond it. I do remember wondering what on earth had possessed me to think I could look after a horse as valuable as Adelfa, why I had started out on this ridiculous journey and what in heaven I could do next. I heard a coach coming down the road and as it came alongside where I was crouching, the driver slammed on the brakes and the door opened. Out came an English tourist, wearing a sort of aura of alcohol fumes that preceded him. "Are you alright, mate? Do you speak English? Is that really a horse lying there?" he asked in rapid succession if not very clearly.

"Yes it's a horse and for some reason, she's collapsed and I desperately need help," I gibbered.

"You'll not get a crane out 'ere at this time of night," he replied, stating I felt, the obvious. "We'll have to see what we can do." He turned and leaned back into the coach. "'ere everybody, bloke 'eres got a rorse and it's collapsed and 'e needs a hand."

I found myself surrounded by about 60 English tourists and a bewildered Spanish coach driver. "*Señor*," the small, moustachioed man asked urgently, "do you speaking Spanish?" He was clearly upset at having his routine disturbed and he was hopping anxiously from foot to foot.

"*Si, si entiendo Español.*"

"*Gracias a dios*, what has happened? Is it your horse?"

I explained about the journey, the need for another tranquiliser shot and where I was heading. I was interrupted by my English friend. "Do you want 'er out of the ditch, mate? Or is she staying there for the night?" He giggled at the concept of a horse snoozing quietly in a ditch.

"Er yes, I do want her out of there. But I can't imagine how we can do it," I replied

"Don't you worry. Right, come on everybody. Get round the 'orse and we'll see if we can lift 'er out."

Some 60 tourists who were clearly feeling no pain after a night out at a barbecue gathered around Adelfa. Some jumped down into the ditch and supported her head, others got round her sides and hindquarters and with a lot of hooting and outright laughter, my beloved horse began to arise from where she had lain trapped like Venus stuck in the foam. My helpers placed her gently on her side and Adelfa let out what sounded very like a deep and resonant snore. This caused another outbreak of hysterics among my new-found companions. "'ere," said a woman with the blondest hair I'd ever seen, "she's just been 'avin' a kip – sounds like my old man. Looks like she's 'ad a bit too much as well, same as us."

"Are you alright now, mate?" asked the one who had climbed off the bus first.

"I can't thank you enough," I replied. "I wish I could buy you all a drink."

"Don't worry about that," one of them laughed, "we've got plenty more on the bus." And with that they all got back on board. An arm appeared through a window and handed me an open bottle of red wine. "There you are, dearie," cried a voice, "that'll see you home. You look like a bloke that enjoys a drink. You'll be alright. Good luck with the 'orse." And with a cheer from the assembled company, the driver let out the clutch and the bus set off once more in the direction of Ibiza town.

Again, I found myself alone in the middle of the country with a recumbent horse who was snoring gently, a bottle of wine and no idea how I was going to get home. I sat down by Adelfa's head and started gently stroking her muzzle while at the same time taking swigs from my bottle. Time passed and various night creatures rustled through the dried grasses. A Scops owl landed somewhere nearby and started his gentle hooting and all in all I thought that as long as Adelfa woke up in the not-too-distant future, life could be worse.

❧

Somewhere about 4am, she suddenly lifted her head and peered blearily around. By this time, exhaustion and the wine had made me feel completely knocked out but I scrambled to my feet just as Adelfa lurched upright. Clearly she was feeling much better as she stared into the night before lowering her head to see if there was anything to eat. I took a last swig from the bottle, lifted her reins and tried to encourage her to set off home once more.

She was obviously not too sure about whole thing. Bringing one of her beautiful hooves down very firmly on my right foot, she went back to grazing again and it was some time before I could persuade her that her new abode was just over the hill.

Dawn was well and truly in the sky by the time we reached home. I put her in her freshly prepared stable, fed and watered her and finally limped off to bed. Of course I couldn't sleep so I ran a cool bath and lay there until I felt myself nodding off and I staggered off to bed.

A childhood of asthma had taught me to recover pretty quickly and by the time I woke I was feeling reasonably normal apart from the fact that my foot had swollen to twice its size and I could only just put it down on the ground. Nevertheless, I had a horse to care for and so I went off to her stable only to find her bright eyed and raring to go. I groaned at the thought of mucking her out but it had to be done. I'd decided to use the traditional Ibicenco material for her bedding – seaweed. It's clean, hygienic and what's more, it's free.

The type of seaweed used is that long, flat, single leafed kind that you find piled up by the waves on many Mediterranean beaches. It looks like enormous grey duvets stacked along the coast and all you have to do is to gather it one year, leave it outside for 12 months to allow the rain to wash some of the salt away, and then let it dry. It smells wonderful and horses love it. Many a night I would go into Adelfa's stable and lie down on the mattress of seaweed and she would come and collapse heavily, using me as a convenient pillow.

By this point, my foot was really looking unpleasant, a mixture of black and purple and quite swollen. Obviously I couldn't drive, but fortunately Lynda, who I'd last seen after she got her driving licence, came by just when I was wondering how I could get into town. "Oh what a darling horse," she cooed, as Adelfa stuck her head inquisitively over her stable door. "Isn't she gorgeous? I knew your were getting an Arab, but she's really beautiful. My God," she went on, "you look as though you've been on a bender for the last fortnight. Where have you been? Ooh, and what have you done to your foot?"

"A certain gorgeous horse stamped on it at about 4am this morning," I explained dryly. "I don't suppose there's any chance you could run me into town and wait while I get it X-rayed? I'd buy you lunch in return."

"What girl could resist such an offer. Hop in – oops, sorry darling, wrong thing to say. I can't wait for my lunch, where shall we go?"

Having made Adelfa completely secure, I climbed into Lynda's Citroen Mehari and off we went. The wait in the hospital wasn't too bad and I passed the time describing the last two weeks to Lynda who was suitably sympathetic. Finally a nurse collected me, let out a squeak when she saw my foot and sent me off for an X-ray. Then it was just a question of waiting until a doctor saw me. "Horses are very big and heavy," he said severely, "and the human foot is small. They don't go well together, *Señor*. We cannot set this in plaster but I can tell you that there are two or three small bones which are broken." My glamorous companion who had so far put up the pulse rates of doctors, patients and a male orderly alike put her hand tenderly under my elbow as I hobbled out to the accounts department. Settling up for the treatment was quick and simple, thanks to the system operated by my insurance company. You paid them monthly or annually and they in turn issued you with a book of vouchers. You then handed over however many vouchers were needed to pay for your treatment and the whole process was painless – unlike my foot that had ended up wrapped in a tight elastic bandage. I left the hospital clutching a large packet of painkillers and another of anti-inflammatory pills with the doctor's words ringing in my ears.

As we left the Clinic, the unwilling vet stopped his car in front of us. "*Señor,*" he cried, "what has happened to your feets? You did not have this *anoche*, last night."

I told him about the journey home and Adelfa's strange behaviour, including her collapsing in the road. He paled and stammering, replied, "Ah, this could have been the *tranquilizante* I gave her. She might have reacted badly to the *medicina*." He scratched his head nervously as he thought for a moment and wringing his hands, he came to a decision. "In the circumstances, *Señor* Andersen, you mustn't feel you have to pay me too quickly."

I felt a small explosion next to me as Lynda started to erupt like a miniature volcano. I tried to stop her but it was too late. "Too quickly? What do you mean too quickly? You admit you injected his unbelievably beautiful and valuable horse with a *tranquilizante* to which she might have been allergic and then you talk about him paying you? His foot is broken, maybe his leg also. His life and his horse were in danger. He is a caring man. How dare you talk about him paying you?" Her Spanish became incredibly fluent when roused, in all senses of the word. She had obviously learned it under a number of different circumstances

The vet looked distinctly abashed. "*Señorita*, forgive me, perhaps you have misunderstood. I meant to say that the *Señor* mustn't feel he has to pay me at all." With a final waggle of his moustache, he accelerated rapidly away from the curb leaving me open mouthed with amazement. "I wouldn't have dared to say that to him," I said. "Knowing the old devil, he'd have had the money out of me in the next day or so."

"You won't have to wait that long with me," gurgled Lynda. "We're going to go to Las Almendras for the best lunch they can manage. And after that," she purred seductively, "you might just have to put your foot up on something soft."

19.

Letting the Cat out of the box

About four years after I bought my house in Ibiza, there came a year when the weather was simply awful. There were some weeks when the sun would shine but the temperature never really climbed to the point where you could actually burn yourself lying on the beach. A pleasant rosy glow was the best that most of us could manage and there was a general air of, "Oh Lord, something has gone wrong." Everybody started to feel cranky and there was an uncomfortable sense of malaise.

Even the animals started to get creaky, especially my old Labrador, Angus. He'd moved with me from England and had lived a wonderful life in the sun. But finally he'd reached the end of a long road. His hips started to hurt, from being exceptionally sharp-eyed his eyesight became very poor and his normally hearty appetite diminished. His wonderful blond coat that he had shaken so enthusiastically when he came out of the water after swimming started to look like a tired old hearthrug and at 13 it was no surprise that he was in trouble. The truth was that I should have recognised the inevitable two years before. We have a huge responsibility to the animals that live with us and certainly in my case it was sheer cowardice that I hadn't taken matters in hand before.

The decision was made one evening when I realised he was fighting to stand up but failing to lever himself onto his tired old legs. The dignity of this amazing old friend was astonishing but I knew that something major had happened, possibly a stroke, and that his time had come. I went and phoned my vet from a call box. Young and really caring, Toni had a special quality with animals. He was the new breed of Spaniard who felt that animals weren't put on the earth simply to work for us. This isn't a criticism of the old ways, for in a country where poverty defined so many people's lives, pets were a luxury. Toni was out on an emergency when I called but his wife said she would ask him to come as soon as possible.

I went home and lay down in his bed with Angus. His back legs were flailing and he was unable to control an overall trembling. We stayed like that for some hours, my arms wrapped around him, a blanket over both of us. To try and calm him and in an attempt to give him good memories to take with him on his journey, I told him stories about his life. I reminded him of when we first met, how small he'd been then and how he'd grown so much and become one of the best friends I could ever have had. I talked about how his first entrance into Spain was in a travelling box on the conveyor belt at Barcelona Airport when he was just six months old. He'd flown in the hold of the plane and I reminded him how a *Guardia Civil* had been terrified when I opened the door of the travelling box and out came this large blond Labrador puppy. The *Guardia Civil* had retreated at high speed, nervously fingering his pistol.

I told Angus about the days we'd spent on the beach at Es Pou d'es Llou, how we'd swum together and how he'd towed me by letting me hold on to his tail as he paddled. I also told him how much I enjoyed seeing him dive off rocks into the sea and how funny he was as he tried to snap at passing small fry near the surface. Gradually as I talked, he seemed to become calmer and I repeated how much he'd meant to me, how much his affection had counted in my life and how I had always looked forward to seeing him again each time I'd had to leave him in kennels.

❧

Finally at about 7am, Toni appeared. He examined my old friend and he turned to me, his face sad. "*Lo siento mucho, amigo mio,*" he murmured quietly, "he has had a stroke. It is time to help him on his way."

I nodded my agreement. My voice was too wobbly to say anything as Toni prepared a syringe. Tears ran down my face as he gently inserted the needle and with a sigh, 13 years of Angus's company ended. I thanked Toni for all his kindness and he replied, "*Hombre,* I hate doing that, especially to such a noble animal. Come, I will help you to bury him and then we must have a drink to his memory."

And so the two of us dug a hole in the iron hard earth in the garden, wrapped Angus in blanket and buried him. Then we went back into the house and I opened a bottle of whisky and poured two generous measures. Toni left but I continued in much the same vein for the rest of the day. Needless to say, it left me with a raging hangover by early evening but I thought it was a fitting tribute to a good friend.

My next encounter with Toni the vet occurred when my ginger tom, Tanit, came home late one Saturday night with breathing difficulties. A well-known publisher had employed me to provide the information for a guide book to Ibiza and I'd spent the evening working at home. This had involved the consumption of a certain amount of red wine and so at first I was quite relaxed about things. However, when I listened his breathing sounded more like a pair of leaky bellows than a normal healthy cat and I began to worry. I glanced at my watch and it seemed to say midnight and while I felt bad about disturbing Toni at such a time, I felt I had no choice.

Tanit had a slightly strange character. When he was about eight weeks old and living happily on a building site with his mother and siblings, he was scooped up by some friends who were coming to me for dinner and who believed fervently that because they were cat lovers, the whole world should also adore the feline race. This tiny ginger ball of spitting, biting fluff was deposited with me and gradually we signed a truce. At this point, his teeth weren't quite up to the job of severing my thumb, try as he might, and he learned to enjoy the pleasures of a warm home and regular meals. It may sound fanciful, but I always felt that what really caused my little, but very macho cat, the biggest psychological damage was the fact that I named him after Tanit, the goddess of Ibiza. In a way, perhaps he was always trying to prove that he really was a top cat and not some female who ruled over the island a couple of thousand years ago.

Katherine, who by now had moved in with me, was away and so I was alone in the house. The nearest phone box was about a quarter of a mile away and I jumped in the car and went off to find out if there was any chance of a late night consultation for my cat. I managed to catch Toni at home. "*Hombre*," he murmured somewhat reluctantly, "I could meet you at the surgery in about half an hour if you wish. I will have to get dressed again but that is okay."

I thanked him, hung up, went home and collected the cat box, a towel and so on and set off in the direction of Ibiza town. These days I wouldn't consider driving in such a condition but then I was young and ignorant and thankfully I arrived safely at the main square, collected the paraphernalia off the back seat of the car and walked over to the surgery. The light was on and I rang the bell. He answered almost immediately. "Come in, *amigo mio*," he greeted me warmly. We went into the surgery and he indicated I should put the cat box on the table.

Toni bent down and peered in through the mesh door. He didn't say anything for a moment and then he gave a slight shudder. He turned his head and peered over his shoulder at me. His voice became rather more formal than usual as he said in a grating tone, "*Señor* Stewart, where is the cat?"

I bent down beside him and I too looked inside. To my horror I realised I had managed to bring everything except the cat. My reasonably fluent Spanish flew out of the window as I stuttered an apology. "*Er Toni, lo siento mucho*, I am so sorry. I can't imagine how I did such a stupid thing. I can go back quickly and get the cat."

"I will be back in bed by the time you return," he interrupted dryly. "It will be better if I give you an injection for you to give to the cat – I know what is wrong with him – there are many *gatitos* who have a mild flu at the moment."

I winced at the thought of trying to give an injection. Like many people, I have a dislike of needles and the idea of trying to hold Tanit still while jabbing a syringe full of medicine into him didn't exactly fill me with joy and delight. Clearly though, I had upset Toni enough for one night and so I took the two syringes without a murmur. "The second one is for you to practice with," explained the vet, a certain amount of malicious glee in his voice. "Fill it with water and try injecting it into an orange. You'll soon get the idea. And now, *buenos noches*, I am going home to my wife, my bed and my sleep." With that he ushered me firmly out of the door.

I drove home slowly and thoughtfully. The night sky was the softest velvet and all around me was the scent of pines on a warm night. Instead of being soothed, however, my mind was filled with visions of cat's claws and angry hissings. As a race our feline friends are prone to expressing their feelings rather forcefully and they have about a millisecond of patience for those things that don't attract them. I'd heard about wrapping them in a towel and I had a vision of Katherine returning to find both the towel and me in tatters.

There was no help for it, though, and by the time I arrived home I was in a mood of grim determination and do or die optimism. I had managed to convince myself that he would regard me as his hero and saviour and just for once, he'd call a truce.

I set up my HQ in the kitchen where my small ginger friend was corralled. I unpacked the kit that Toni had handed me. An orange, a glass of water and a large glass of wine came next but not in that order. Feeling very Dr Kildare-ish and rather regretting that I didn't have a white coat, I filled the syringe with water from the glass and then held it up to the light as I'd seen doctors do in order to get rid of any air bubbles which I gathered could do untold harm to the blood stream of human and cat alike. Then I picked up the orange, turned it round in my hand until I found the best spot and stabbed it with the needle, at the same time pressing the plunger.

I heard a sudden intake of breath behind like an old train getting up a head steam. I turned and found a pair of golden green eyes staring fixedly at what I was doing. Tanit resembled nothing so much as my great aunt Hesta when she found I'd hidden an elderly herring that I'd found on Bognor beach under her mattress. The herring was definitely the worse for wear and so was I by the time Hesta's firm right hand had finished with me.

Tanit seemed to be sending me the same message: "Mess with me, sonny and you'll regret it." He turned on one of his four heels and swept out of the kitchen through the cat flap that I'd carelessly forgotten to lock. In my slightly confused state, I stared after him for some moments. "Come back," I cried but it was useless. He'd gone – leaving, as the poet said, not a wrack nor a wraith behind him. To tell the truth, I'm not sure which of us was the more relieved, Tanit because he had a handy escape route or me because the threat of severe lacerations had been removed from my life and my wrists.

Two days later my large ginger friend returned to the house apparently none the worse for his not quite getting the needle. His breathing was back to normal, time had obviously removed the rift between us and having downed a large bowl of food, he leapt on my lap purring like a lunatic. I, in my turn, did the decent thing and provided a fair amount of scratching behind the ear and tickling under the chin. Never again did I think of injecting anything, let alone an irritable redhead.

20.
The End of an Era

On the morning of 20th November 1975, I opened the shutters and peered out. It was like looking at a white wall that rippled and swirled as I stared into a world shrouded in the densest of mists. Famously fast-moving, the mist, the *boira,* had filled the valley up to the brim. Every branch and leaf was clad in droplets and the damp seemed to creep into each brick of the house. It was the kind of mist that if you were on the road and drove into it, you would simply have to stop and hope that everyone else stopped as well.

Coaxing the embers in the stove into life, they suddenly caught and I added a couple of logs from an old almond tree that had blown down. This was such a sweet smelling wood that there was a temptation to leave the lid off the stove. Fortunately, I had nowhere I needed to go that day and so by mid-morning when I'd completed the usual household chores I settled down in a comfortable chair to work on an article I had to write, a bottle of red wine at my elbow, pad and pen at the ready and my elderly Olivetti portable typewriter to hand. I wanted to finish the article, so while Katherine cooked a chicken casserole which filled the house with the scent of garlic and onions, I got down to work. Suddenly, there was a knock on the door and an urgent cry of "*Oiga, amigo Eduardo,*" came from outside. It was Francisco who lived nearby.

"*Pase, amigo mio,*" I answered.

He came in with an anxious look on his tanned face, his eyes as round as saucers. "Señor, have you listened to the news this morning on your radio?"

"No, no, there's never any good news," I laughed.

"*Pero Señor*, they tell me that, well, there is a rumour that, well, *Vd se sabe*, you know," he stammered, "you know, you have heard that *el Caudillo, Señor* Franco has been unwell?"

"Yes, so I'd heard," I replied.

"Well, *amigo mio*," he went on, his voice sinking to a whisper, "there is a rumour that he is dead."

"*No me diga*," I exclaimed, "are you serious? Dead? Well, he's had a pretty good run for his money and we've all got to go sometime."

"*Señor*, please, don't joke about it. Never in my whole life have I been more serious," he responded. "You didn't live here during the *Guerra Civil* – it was a bad time and nobody knows what will happen now. We must pray that violence doesn't return to *España*. I don't have a radio but you have one. Could we perhaps listen and see if there is any news from Madrid? This is a very serious day."

I went into the kitchen and told Katherine about the rumour and she immediately came in, said "*Buenos dias*" to Francisco and turned on the radio to the BBC World Service. Along with so many other people in a multitude of countries, if we wanted to know exactly what was happening, we turned without fail to the World Service. Being of great good sense, she also went back to the kitchen, put on the kettle to make coffee and returned with three glasses and a bottle of 103 Brandy.

"*Caray, Señores, que buen idea*, what a good idea," exclaimed our guest who was momentarily distracted from the business of the day and whose mood lifted for the first time since he walked in the door.

We listened to the news and translated for Francisco at the same time. When we'd heard a complete news bulletin that described the swearing in of the new King, we turned to *Radio Nacional* and listened to their broadcast in Spanish. Francisco looked even more nervous as he heard the news in his own language.

"This could be the start of big *problemas, Señores*," he said gravely. "If the *Franquistas* or the *Communistas* decide to make trouble, there could be revolution, and as I say, perhaps even a return to the *Guerra Civil*, the civil war. It was such a terrible time, you cannot imagine." His anxious face made me realise how seriously people took this transition of power and suddenly it appeared that our paradise might be in serious danger of collapsing around our ears. Some time before, I'd read *The Life and Death of a Spanish Town* by American journalist Elliot Paul written when he had lived in Santa Eulalia during the Civil War. This was a powerful book that was handed around under plain cover with great care in my early years in Ibiza. Owning and reading it was definitely frowned on by the authorities. In it, Paul described how he had lived in my local village of Santa Eulalia from about 1931 until the start of the War and how he had managed to get out in 1936. He talked about some of the terrible things that happened and how awful conditions became on the island.

Could life in Spain ever return to that with brother fighting brother? Was it really possible after all the terrible times of the Spanish Civil War and World War II that such insanity could happen yet again? I found it hard to believe but one look at Francisco's ashen face made me realise that, certainly in the minds of some Spaniards, it was a definite possibility. Ibicencos have always been an independent people who prefer to stand on their own two feet and they have never liked being told what to do. Could democracy gain a permanent foothold in Spain now that *el caudillo* had gone or would Left fight Right once more? We just had to hope that democracy would be triumphant and that wiser heads could steer the country through difficult times.

Some three decades later, I met a man in Mallorca who spoke the local dialect with a distinctly mainland accent. We started talking and I asked him how long he'd been on the island. "*Señor,*" he replied, "I have been here since the day after *el Caudillo*, Franco died. I used to own a factory on the mainland, but once he had gone, the left-wing workers started to come in. I wanted nothing of it so I took my money, handed the keys of the factory to them and I left." This was the depth of feeling that existed around the time of Franco's death and I think many of us who were young then, grew up a little with the realisation that such terrible things had happened right where we were living. None of the changes that have occurred since the end of the '70s had taken place then and thankfully democracy has found good soil in which to take root in Spain.

Francisco stayed for another hour and we discussed all the momentous changes that could possibly occur. At the same time, we abandoned the coffee and stayed with brandy. The mist had cleared leaving a rather shamefaced watery blue sky and dripping wet pine trees and we felt that perhaps the clearing of the weather was an omen for the future. Finally he took his leave, weaving slightly. His parting shot was, "Whatever happens, you will always be welcome in my house *Señores*." He tottered down the stairs, tried to walk through the closed garden gate, finally figured out that he had to open it and disappeared in the direction of his house.

I suggested to Katherine that maybe we should cancel our trip to Palma and wait for a more auspicious time, but she had set her heart on going. The following morning we set off to the airport, and, having left the car in the part of the car park reserved for the staff who ran the Control Tower, we bought every newspaper available. Needless to say, they were full of what was happening in Madrid as well as comments from around the world about the situation in Spain. It seemed as though journalists from every newspaper, radio and television station from countries around the world had invaded the Spanish capital and they carried column after column of quotes from senior politicians, junior politicians, in fact everyone including road sweepers and bar tenders. We realised that living in Ibiza had largely insulated us from the world with a gentle cushion that made the world seem a kindlier place than it actually was. The proverbial cold wind was blowing round us and it came as a shock as we sat on the Iberia plane to Ibiza's sister island. We held hands and wondered what would happen next to our neat, safe little world. Perhaps it was the first time we had realised that we had been naïve in believing we could escape from reality.

It's amazing how life turns and turns. About 15 years later I sat in Richmond Theatre on the outskirts of London and enjoyed Peter Ustinov's one man show. In it, he told the story of how, when Francisco Franco was lying in a coma in the Palace in Madrid and nearing death, a crowd was gathering outside in the streets. As Franco's wife came into the room, her husband came out of the coma. Hearing the tumult from outside he asked his wife, "What is that noise?"

"It is the people of Spain, they have come to say goodbye," she replied.

"Where are they going?" asked Franco.

&

The reason for our trip was twofold. Christmas was coming and we'd found a German butcher in Palma who did the most wonderful hams, real English sausages and smoked bacon and was prepared to take orders and ship to us in Ibiza in time for the festivities.

The real reason though was that Adelfa had refused to consider the handsome stallion to whom she'd been introduced in Ibiza and we were going to Mallorca to meet an Arab horse breeder who lived at the northern end of the island. She had a stallion, so it was rumoured, that no mare could resist. Fingers crossed, we thought, that our mare would find him an absolute dish and that we'd soon be godparents to a sprightly little version of Adelfa.

Having gone via the butcher and ordered far too much food to be forwarded on to us, we found ourselves in the main square of the town of Pollensa. By now it was approaching lunchtime and we were both hungry and thirsty. Lisa, the American Arab-horse breeder who had her farm near the town and who owned SZED Arabians, had previously agreed to join us there and we decided to make the most of a bar in the main square of Pollensa on the side next to the church. The aromas of the cooking were like an especially refined form of torture and we quickly ordered wine, *aceitunas* or olives, bread and *ali-y-olli*. Katherine had *tortilla Española* and a salad and I had wonderful grilled sardines, *patatas fritas* and a delicious *ensalada mixta*. For pudding we both devoured an ice cream. While Lisa and I had coffees and a cognac each, Katherine had spotted a machine on the bar that seemed to be stirring what looked to me like dark liquid mud but which turned out to be hot liquid chocolate. She spooned down a cup-full while, after dissecting the previous day's news from Madrid with Lisa, we discussed her stallion, his prowess and where we should go from here.

At the end of lunch, we followed Lisa's car and went off to see her farm that nestled in a valley behind Pollensa. There was a definite feeling of California about the place with the long low house, the modern kitchen, the enormous fireplace and large, comfortable furniture. There we were introduced to her small herd of mares who all came and clustered around the fence looking for hands to stroke their muzzles, and pockets in which treats might just be lurking. Lisa had given us pieces of apple but warned us to save some for her stallion, Ibn Saud. Apparently few things pleased him more and whether his sense of smell told him what we were feeding his harem or whether he was psychic, a crash followed by a high-pitched snickering told us that he was getting impatient.

We walked round the side of the stable block and there was the most gorgeous dark bay head sticking out over his stable door. Ibn Saud was a pure Polish-Arabian stallion Lisa had imported from Germany who gleamed with health and energy. Overall, he was a beautiful, shimmering blood red with black points and he had the most elegant and superbly shaped head.

His bloodline was about as good as you could get and obviously he knew it. But at the moment it was clear that there was only one thing this king among horses wanted. He was dancing from foot to foot in anticipation and if he could have climbed over the bottom half of the door, he would. Lisa went over and held a piece of apple up in her fingers while at the same time she whispered quietly in his ear. Ibn Saud pulled back his lips and carefully took the fruit in his teeth. A look of bliss came over his face as he chewed and scrunched the fruit carefully but then he noticed I had something similar in my hand. He quickly swallowed his mouthful and stretched his head out to greet me. Obviously this could have gone on all afternoon as far as he was concerned but Lisa had other ideas.

She slipped into the stable, put a head collar on Ibn Saud, clipped on a leading-rein and led him outside. He glanced hopefully in my direction but when he realised that treat time was over, his head went up and he followed in Lisa's wake with that incredibly springy step that is so typical of an Arab horse. Opening a gate, Lisa took him into a large *paradero*, a fenced-off cross between a field and a lawn and with a click of the tongue, she started lunging him in ever-widening circles around her. Quite simply, he was glorious, proud without being arrogant and quite aware that we were there to provide him with what he wanted.

Hopefully, little Adelfa would behave properly in front of what potentially could be her lord and master because it was quite clear that shortly she would be heading from Ibiza to Pollensa to meet Ibn Saud. We sorted out the details with Lisa of when and how our little mare would arrive in Mallorca. Lisa dropped us back to Pollensa and we drove our hire car back to the airport outside Palma. Somehow, spending time with such a beautiful creature had wiped all the negative thoughts of the last 24 hours from our minds and we flew home in a far better frame of mind.

21.
Calling Out

Everyday things that you took for granted in Britain became a major operation in Ibiza. One of the worst was making a phone call in the early days of my life on the island. Nowadays, we're all so used to mobiles that can be used to ring to and from any continent, as well as faxes, e-mails and modems; we tend to forget that only thirty years ago phones were a rarity in places such as Ibiza. The concept of having one in your house hadn't arrived anywhere near me and phone boxes were unheard of. To make a call, you went either to the larger *Telefonica* in Ibiza or to the much smaller one in Santa Eulalia.

Phoning within Spain was one thing, but phoning abroad required language skills that I certainly didn't possess at the outset. If the operator couldn't, wouldn't or didn't understand the name of the place you were trying to call, you were required to spell it out in the Spanish version of Alpha, Bravo, Charlie, Delta and so on. I found in my primitive Spanish the magic word *deletrear*, to spell, and by saying the phrase, "*lo deletrea para Vd*," firmly and in a manner that indicated that I knew what on earth I was talking about, generally I'd manage to get what I wanted across to the patient operator at the other end of the line. So asking for a number in, for example, London or *Londres* required me to say, "*Lerida, Oviedo, Navarra, Domingo, Ramón, Enrique, Sabado*." These weren't the correct words for the letters but they were usually the only ones I could think of at the time.

Even worse was making a reverse charge call. Only once did I try to call my aunt Marjorie *cobro revertido*. The process involved giving the number you required and your name to the operator sitting in front of you in the *Telefonica* and then sitting down and waiting for anything up to two hours if it was a busy time. You couldn't leave even for a second, because if you were called and you weren't there, you lost your place in the queue. Eventually you'd be told which was your *cabina*. You picked up the phone and listened to another operator trying to make the connection. On this particular occasion, I heard the phone ring in London and my aunt answer.

"Hello," she said cautiously.

"*Buenos noches*," replied the operator. He continued in English, "*Señor* Andersen is calling you from Ibiza. Will you accept the charges?"

Admittedly his accent was somewhat thick but at least that's what I heard. What reached my beloved aunt was obviously something different, because instead of her pleasant, giggly voice, all I heard was her saying sharply to the operator, "You disgusting little man, how dare you ask me such a thing, you should be reported to the authorities," and the sound of her banging the phone down. You then had two options under the circumstances. The first was to ask the operator to try again, which could mean waiting for another two hours or the second which was to give up entirely and go to the nearest bar for a drink.

In Santa Eulalia there were only two phones in the *Telefonica* that was run usually by a pleasant but slightly vague girl who spent far more time reading a copy of *Hola* magazine from cover to cover. Sundays were especially busy for her because that was when soldiers from the barracks outside Ibiza town might well arrive in a group of anything up to ten at a time with the intention of phoning home to their parents. They were out of uniform and they appeared to be just an ordinary group of young Spanish men from different parts of the country having a day out. The waiting involved a great deal of pushing, shoving, giggling, nudging and pointing at the operator, who ignored them completely in favour of her magazine or painting extremely small, silver stars on her very dark nail varnish.

As new customers arrived, she would take down the number they wanted and they would then join the queue. From time to time the phone in one of the boxes would ring and the operator would call out the number that was on line. When it was one of the soldiers, a dramatic transformation would come over the individual. Gone would be the laughing young man and in his place would stand a dramatic figure straight out of an operatic tragedy. He would enter the box, carefully shut the door which was a complete waste of time as the rest of us could hear every word he said, pick up the receiver and instantly sob, "*Mama, mama, te quiero mama.*" Roughly translated, this meant, "Mama, mama, I love you and miss you and your cooking and besides, my friends are listening to this and I know they'll do the same when it's their turn and anyway, if I don't make this pretty good, you'll give me a verbal clip round the ear. Oh, and by the way, how's papa and my sisters and brothers?" This would go on for between five and ten minutes and with a final burst of, "*adios, mama, te quiero, adios, adios*" our hero would carefully hang up and emerge looking slightly sheepish while brushing at his eyes with his sleeve. His *compañeros* would be waiting for him and once again there would be several minutes of backslapping and sniggering. Once they'd all finished, of course, they'd be off to a bar and admiring *las señoritas extranjeras*, the foreign girls.

When my turn came and the operator called out, "*Londres,*" there would be a general round of nudging each other and mutters of, "*Eh, Londres, el señor va hablar con Londres,* he's going to speak to London." Once in a while, you'd hear a voice raised in surprise that London wasn't in Spain and that I wasn't talking to my mama. However, a respectful silence would descend on the assembled community while I made my call.

The day came when I had to ring Lisa to confirm the impending arrival of Adelfa in Mallorca. Katherine and I drove to Santa Eulalia and I parked behind the *Ayuntamiento*, the Town Hall. It was a hot and airless afternoon and the idea of being stuck in the airless little office for hours didn't really appeal but it had to be done. Katherine went off to find us a couple of bottles of cold beer and I entered the *Telefonica*. For a few moments I stood there while my eyes adapted to the shade.

I realised with a start that I was the only customer and this was like being handed a huge gift. The idea of not having to wait for ages was wonderful, and as long as Lisa was at home the call should go through quite smoothly. After the obligatory 15 minutes, I was summoned to the *cabina* and there was Lisa. "You're really bringing her?" she asked happily and I confirmed that in two weeks time, we'd be on the quayside in Palma plus one horse. "I'll bring my trailer and we'll take her up to the farm in that," she said. We made some final arrangements and I hung up.

At that moment, Katherine came back with the beers and we wandered down the main *paseo* to the sea to drink them. We had a lot to plan, not least the fact that Adelfa had to be moved from Antonio the taxi driver's farm, where she'd been having a change of scene, down to the port. We decided that it was too complex to try and find a suitable trailer in Ibiza to move her and eventually we agreed that Katherine would drive me to Antonio's *finca* and then go home. I, in the meantime would set out walking our incredibly valuable mare down the network of *caminos* towards the Port in Ibiza. It was a mere 15 kilometres and I guessed that she'd be quite tired once we arrived in town. In the meantime, Katherine would drive into Ibiza, park the car and meet me somewhere near the ship.

The next day, I drove over to meet Antonio to tell him about the arrangements. He agreed that it seemed the most sensible way of doing things – but when I suggested that he might care to join me on a 16-kilometre hike he rapidly found he had something else to do that day. Clearly a *taxista* didn't walk that kind of distance for anybody.

22.
Cheesed Off

Collecting your post involved the not-too-arduous task of driving into, in my case, Ibiza town, going to the *Correos*, the Post Office and checking in your *apartado*, your mail box to see if anything had survived the arduous journey from another country to Spain, then to Ibiza and finally into your *apartado*. There was a kind of childlike surprise, a feeling of Christmas, about finding something that had actually made it. Even better was when there was a slip of paper with a reference number that indicated the recipient should go to the counter and pick up a package.

I was surprised one morning to receive a letter from the father of a friend of mine, Peter. I'd helped him out with some translation and in return, so his letter said, he was sending me a Fortnum & Mason Stilton. When we met originally over dinner, we'd discussed food in general and in particular, cheese which we both enjoyed very much. We'd agreed that our dinner that evening would have been perfect if we could have rounded it off with a good piece of Stilton and a glass of port. In fact, I remembered waxing lyrical about it.

I also remembered pointing out that doubtless I could find a bottle of port in Ibiza but Stilton didn't exist. Well, here was a promise of a whole one and my excitement was intense. Hurriedly, I checked the date the letter had been sent – 29th September. It was the 15th October but there was no sign of it arriving yet. I went over to the counter and explained that a parcel should have arrived and I gave them the Fortnum & Mason details as well as those of Peter's father.

Juan, who worked behind the counter, went off and had a desultory prod at a mound of packages that reclined in a corner. "No *Señor*," he said with a weary shrug of his shoulders as he strolled back with his hands in his trouser pockets, "*no hay ningun paquete para Usted,* nothing for you today."

"*Bueno*, I'll come back tomorrow," I replied. Two weeks should have been enough time for the package to arrive. Maybe I was wrong but I'd started to worry about the condition of my precious cheese.

As a consolation prize, I went round to the Vara de Rey to have a drink. I was walking past a bar deep in thought when, from a table outside came a loud shriek of a voice that I remembered only too well. "Hello, coooeee, it's me, Winifred, and Simon's come to join me out here and I've brought some of my teddies out for lunch and to have a little drinky, Simon would love to meet you, you can sit down and have lunch with us, we've bought a house near Santa Eulalia and we're moving in soon."

At other tables, startled Ibicencos stared wildly round them, fixing their gaze finally on Winifred. One or two hurriedly paid for their drinks and left while the rather more hardy ones glared at Winifred, took a long pull on their drinks and went back to reading the *Diario de Ibiza*.

"Simon, this is my friend from the hotel that I told you, the one who wasn't well and I volunteered to give the bits that were sore a soothing rub, his chest I mean," she squealed coquettishly, "but he went off with not so much as a goodbye kiss, I wouldn't have eaten him up, would I, well not more than 'alf."

More Ibicencos were leaving the bar and I could see the owner wringing his hands as his profit disappeared with them. I now knew what a large fish feels when it's been hooked and is being reeled in to an unpleasant fate worse than death. I went over to the table where Winifred was sitting with a young man with a vacuous smile on his face.

"Er, hello," I said, wishing I was on the other side of the world and wondering why on earth I'd gone for a drink. "How nice to see you. It's been ages." I started to retreat backwards from the table when Winifred leapt up like an anxious trout after a particularly tempting fly. "You come and sit down, I've ever so much to tell you, it's been ages since we last met, at least three or four years, but I'd have known you anywhere, Simon wouldn't though, he's never met you before, say hello Simon."

"Er, 'ello, I'm Simon," he said in a subdued voice, as he bobbed up, shook my hand with his rather clammy one, and then relapsed into a dazed silence again.

"You come and sit down, we must catch up and the bears want to meet you formally, they never did meet you that night in the hotel, they were so disappointed, what'll you have?"

"*Una caña, por favor,* a beer," I muttered to the waiter, hoping against hope he wouldn't think they were close friends of mine.

"Oooh listen Simon, he's totally fluent in *el* jolly old *Español,* you never mentioned you spoke the lingo that night we spent together, pardon my French but you know what I mean, you'll be ever so useful to us now we're moving in, don't you agree, all those solicitors and notary things we've got to do and there'll be lots of things for the house I'll need you for, I can really make use of you," she said in the vague direction of the edge of the table. A bear's head peered over the edge of the table and Winifred muttered in what she thought was a bear's voice, "He certainly will be useful, now he's a close friend of ours."

The bear's head shot down again and Winifred continued, "You must come to dinner on Thursday night, bring a friend, bring as many friends as you like, we always keep open house, and then we can discuss one or two little things I'd like you to start helping us with."

"Ah well, you see, much as I'd love too, I'm catching a boat to Mallorca for some time but I'll be glad to look you up when I get back. Well, it's been lovely seeing you," I went on, backing away from the table. "Must dash!"

"Just a minute, 'ang on," cried Winifred in the tone of a lioness who has just missed catching her evening meal, "off to Mallorca you may be, but you disappeared from my life once, I'm not having it again, where do you live and how can I contact you, I want to keep in touch with you."

"Ah well, you see, I live out in the sticks, you'd never find it but most days you can find me at this bar after I've picked up my post. Now, I must fly," I said, leaving the money for my caña on the table.

"You just said you were catching a boat to Mallorca, now you say you're going to fly," said Simon in a surly voice.

"Oooh he's sharp is our Simon," added Winifred, "now which is it deary, boat or plane, on second thoughts we'll come and see you off at the harbour or the airport, whichever it is." She started to gather her things up and indicated to the waiter that he should give me the bill for everybody.

At that moment, salvation in divine form appeared. Our friend Lynda, who I hadn't seen for some time, pulled up at the curb and I went over to her car. "Darling," she murmured seductively, I haven't seen you in ages. Where have you been? How are you? And who are your weird friends? You do consort with the oddest looking people," she giggled. I recognised salvation when I saw it and running round to the passenger side I flung open the door, waved at Winifred and Simon, called out, "Must run!" waved goodbye again, leapt into the car and muttered to Lynda, "Drive off as fast as you can, quickly."

"Oh darling," gurgled Lynda, "you're so masterful. I'm at your command." And with that, she drove off, just barely managing not to stall the car. "Dear heart, what was all that about? And was that a bear I saw in that woman's hand. It seemed to be waving goodbye at us. You really do have some, well, unusual friends."

I sank back in the seat in relief. "Where are you heading now?" I asked her. "Same place as you," she replied. "Lunch. I think I just saved you from a fate worse than death and I claim my reward. Come on, tell me all."

We drove out to Santa Ines to the bar where I knew they did wonderful omelettes, *patatas fritas*, an excellent salad and really cold white wine. It took a while to get there but neither of us were in a hurry and I related my escape from a fate worse than death.

"You don't mean to say she fancied you?" asked Lynda. "My God, you must be hard up if you're consorting with her."

"Well, I think she did. She kept saying she wanted to rub something on my chest, and she tried my bedroom door handle and she keeps on making suggestive remarks. Maybe she wanted to mother me"

Lydia grinned. "There are plenty of others that want that role."

After a long and leisurely lunch, she drove me back into Ibiza to pick up my car. "Avoid the Vara de Rey like the plague in case they're still there," I said, sinking lower into the seat in case we passed Winifred and Simon and a troop of bears. I hopped out of the car and shot into mine like a homing pigeon. I drove home still slumped in my seat, wearing dark glasses and a straw hat someone had forgotten.

The days went past and there was no sign of my Stilton. Juan of the *Correos* clearly got bored with my asking for it and eventually, it slipped out of my mind as well.

Christmas came and went and I thought wistfully but briefly about how pleasant it would have been to have a piece of Stilton on Christmas Day. And then, one day in mid-January, there was a slip in my Apartado telling me I had a package. It seemed a mystery, given that I hadn't ordered anything but I got in the queue and waited my turn. Quite often you were offered packages that had nothing whatsoever to do with you and then you were left with the complicated business of explaining that it actually belonged to someone else. Quite often, Juan or his colleagues would look disappointed that you'd refused their offering.

On this occasion, Juan took the slip of paper, peered at it and it was as though the proverbial light bulb had gone on over his head. He disappeared into a back office and reappeared with a somewhat damaged looking parcel that he placed on the counter. I checked that it had my name on the label, signed for it and then peered at the various labels and stamps, one of which had been franked on 28th September, that were stuck all over it. Underneath something said it had been cleared by the *Aduanas*, the Customs, was the corner of another label that I could just see bore the magic word, 'Fortnum'.

Too excited to wait till I got home, I borrowed a pair of scissors from behind the counter, cut the string and tore off the wrapping paper. Inside was a battered looking box with something squishy inside. "This can't be my wonderful Stilton," I thought disappointedly as I opened the box. Again there was more wrapping.

And then, what seemed quite possibly the worst smell in the world hit me and I have to say, all those round me. It was like all the sewers in the world rolled into one. Juan and his cohorts took several steps backwards as though I'd made a threatening gesture and covering theirs mouth, indicated I should take the parcel outside. Several people who'd been queuing nearby brought their arms up quickly to protect their faces and started coughing as they too backed away.

Suddenly I became deeply annoyed with the whole system. Peter's father had gone to all the trouble of sending me a wonderful gift and someone was responsible for it having been delayed for three months. Using the scissors to good effect, I cut and tore through the last folds of paper. It says much for Fortnum & Masons' wrapping that it had lasted all that time. Out poured one of the most disgusting sights I'd ever seen. The previous smell was as nothing compared with what now happened. Suddenly people decided to collect their mail another day, and that they had an urgent appointment elsewhere.

Juan started yelling at me to take the package away, just as I realised that the box was home to several maggots. "Where do you think I should take it to?" I yelled back. "Is it my fault that 90 days have passed since it was posted in England, why has it taken so long, someone paid a lot of money for this, who is responsible for the problem?" By now I was beginning to sound like Winifred.

In desperation, Juan ordered one of his staff to take it outside the back of the post office to the *basura*, the rubbish bin. The lad promptly refused and in the end, I said, "Let me through and I'll do it." Juan then debated with himself about whether it was better that I should be allowed into his inner sanctum or whether he should carry the package himself. In the end, he gave in and opened a flap in the counter. Indicating that I should follow him, he flung open various doors until we were outside. There stood a large bin. Whipping the lid off with one hand and holding his nose with the other, he indicated that I should drop it inside. Quickly, as though the remains of the package contained marauding hordes of maggots, he slammed the lid down, turned to me, shook his finger angrily and grated, "Don't ever bring anything like that in the *Correos* ever again."

There wasn't much left to say so I made my way back to the front of the *Correos*. "What a day," I thought. "With the way things are going, I'll probably run into Winifred and Simon again."

23.
An Old Friend Leaves Us

We hadn't seen Pierre for some time but one day Katherine and I were having a drink on the terrace of the Hotel Montesol when he came past carrying large tins of black matt paint. Staggering to a halt, he smiled a weary greeting, plonked the paint tins down and dropped gracefully into a chair. *"Bonjour mes amis,"* he explained, "I am quite exhausted. I have been doing up my *finca* and you have no idea how tiring it is."

At that moment, a waiter came over to see what Pierre would have.

"I would very much like a bottle of cold, dry white wine if you two will share it with me?"

"Thank you, we'd love to. Now tell me, you haven't been doing your house up by yourself, have you?" asked Katherine. "It's so big, I'm not surprised you're tired."

"Perhaps I'm getting old," he laughed. "I find that after a day up a ladder, I have to lie down and rest before I go out for dinner."

"I don't want to think what you're doing spending a whole day at the top of a ladder, Pierre," laughed Katherine. "Just what are you up to?"

"Well you see, I have these wonderful ceilings made from beams and the small pieces of wood that rest on them but the paint they are covered in is old and since I bought the house I noticed that small pieces of the paint are falling like black snow flakes. I have been, 'ow you say, scrapping the paint?"

"I think you mean scraping, Pierre, although I guess you could say you're scrapping the old paint by scraping it off and by the sound of it, you're just about ready to start repainting the beams. So why haven't you asked us to help you?" asked Katherine.

"Yes," I agreed, "we'd love to give you a hand. Tell you what, why don't we round up a few friends and make a day of it?"

"My dears, I would be so grateful but do you really mean it? The job has become much more than I thought when I started out; it's almost too much for me. In the meantime," he twinkled happily, "will you join me for lunch now? We must fortify ourselves for the coming battle – whenever it is to be! And I hope you are not planning to do anything else this afternoon. We will enjoy ourselves, and eat and drink until we are filled up." His gestures had become somewhat expansive as the wine slipped down fairly fast.

"Maybe we should make a move to somewhere we can eat," I suggested. "How about strolling into La Marina and see what we can find?"

"It's a good idea, *mon ami*, but I have these with me," he replied indicating the tins of paint. "They are not made for strolling around, believe me. I was going to catch the bus home later on."

I was puzzled that he needed to take the bus, given the smart car that he usually drove. Finally, however, it was decided that I'd go round the corner to my car, put them in the boot and then later, we could drive our friend home. We'd been to buy firewood that morning so it meant that we'd have to squash the three of us in the front but that wasn't a problem.

Lunch at the Delfin Verde on the port, as usual, lasted into the late afternoon and by the time we got Pierre home it was 5.30pm. The only problem with having a house in the country was that to get there you usually had to drive down a pretty rough *camino* and this was no different. With three adults and a load of firewood on board it made the journey especially tricky. "*Mon Dieu,*" panted our friend as we arrived at the house, "this is too much for me. I am become an old man." He turned the enormous key in the lock and we entered what had the potential to become a very beautiful home.

Pierre had bought it in a condition that estate agents describe as 'needing some restoration', which meant that precious little had been done to it for the last 50 years. There was some rudimentary wiring, a bare bulb or two, a couple of taps in the kitchen that emitted rusty water, a lavatory without a door and one of the strange sit-up half baths of the kind that I'd encountered in my San Antonio hotel on my very first night in Ibiza. The house itself was still very beautiful but there was an awful lot of work to do.

We followed Pierre into the kitchen and he indicated where he'd been at work on the ceiling. It was as though a mouse had been scratching at it. I suppose I'd never thought about Pierre's age before but now I looked at him afresh and I realised just how difficult all this could well be for him. I guessed he was 60 plus years old and not in the best of health.

Also, he'd bought the house in the summer about 15 months ago when the metre-thick walls would have kept the house wonderfully cool, but now there was a definite smell of damp in the air and the house was distinctly chilly. I bent down and felt the floor tiles and there was a dead cold to them. During the day it wouldn't have been too bad but once the sun went down, the air would become frigid and the chill would creep back into your bones. I recalled bumping into him when we'd both gone to buy logs and also when he came to my house for the launching of my new chimney. At the time, he'd seemed thrilled with his new purchase but now I wondered whether it was all too much for him.

There was a chimney in the kitchen but I couldn't see any sign of logs. "Have you any firewood, Pierre?" I asked.

"No, no," he replied, looking around him as though he'd mislaid a couple of logs. "I couldn't be bothered to buy any today and it seemed so lovely and warm this morning. Perhaps it is a little chilly now. Never mind, I can get some tomorrow."

"No, you won't wait till tomorrow," Katherine said decisively. "We've a car full of the stuff. You'll have some of ours. We'll bring the car up to the front door and off-load some." I indicated behind Pierre's back that I'd go off and get the car while she talked to him. A few minutes later we were stacking logs around his fireplace. While I'd gone outside, Katherine had laid the fire using an old newspaper and some bits of kindling which was all Pierre had left of his stock of wood. Soon the fire had started to throw heat out into the room and you could feel the cold being driven out. "I would very much like to offer you a drink," Pierre suggested a little awkwardly, "but I'm afraid I seem to have run out."

Katherine interrupted him. "Pierre, you very kindly invited us to lunch today. I don't know how to ask this but I want you to tell me something. Are you having problems with money? Is the house one of the problems? Paying for lunch was one of the problems, wasn't it?"

For a moment, Pierre looked away. He turned back and muttered, "I've found things a little too much for me. The house is costing rather more than I thought to do up. I am a little tired and at my age I don't quite know how to cope. I just thought we would have fun at lunchtime."

"You often joke about your age. Can I ask how old you are?" I asked quietly.

"I'll be 72 at my next birthday," he replied hesitantly.

This was the first time we'd really talked with him. It was different from the kind of restaurant chatter of lunchtime and with the heat beginning to spread through the room, he was relaxing. But I was concerned about how much food he actually had in the house. I went through to the kitchen and found precious little in the cupboards. There was a half empty jar of coffee, some stale bread, biscuits and not a lot else. Clearly a 'care package' was essential, urgently, and I knew there was a *tienda,* a local shop, on the main road that would still be open, so I left Katherine and Pierre talking and slipped out to go and collect some provisions for him.

Half an hour later I arrived back with my *cesta,* that invaluable straw basket that everyone carried on their shoulders, full of food. In another bag, I had a bottle of 103 Brandy, one of Mari Mayans Hierbas, a bottle of olive oil, a couple of bottles of inexpensive wine and a large *pan payes* under my arm.

I found that *hierbas* is one of those drinks that you need to sample a few times before you really get accustomed to it, especially if you're not overly-enthusiastic about sweet drinks. Made from a mixture of things such as thyme, aniseed, rosemary, citrus peel and a few other things that depend on tradition and whose grandmother you listen to, it's said that *hierbas* has curative powers. Certainly it makes an excellent *digestif,* but I found that a couple too many and you're likely to wake up with what feels like a small man with a large mallet attempting to hammer his way out of your skull. I'd brought back the bottle of brandy in the hope that it might warm our friend up. It was certainly something we all turned to in times of crisis.

In my pocket there was a packet of Fortuna cigarettes for Pierre. I found a box of matches, lit his Fortuna, went in to the kitchen, poured us all a 103 brandy and put a pan full of water on the stove. It took just a few moments to chop up some garlic, onions, tomatoes, peppers and some basil and to make a quick basic sauce for pasta.

The quality of the fruit and vegetables even from a small store outshone anything you could get back in England. I knew from visits to the UK just how boring they were in supermarkets, as though they'd all poured out of a machine, and these were so full of flavour, you just knew they were good for you. I'd bought some *chorizo* and cut it into chunks and added it to the sauce. It wasn't exactly *haute cuisine*, but I thought it might do our friend some good.

By now Katherine and Pierre had laid a small table near the chimney and the intoxicating smell of garlic and onions immediately made the house feel more cheerful. Pierre had gone from looking thoroughly embarrassed to feeling no pain as the alcohol took effect.

It seemed important to get to bottom of what had been going on so, as I opened the bottle of red wine, I asked Pierre, "What's been the problem? It seems as if you've haven't been looking after yourself too well."

For a moment, he peered into his glass and then, with an enormous sigh, he said, "It's been a succession of things. First I had money troubles when an investment from which I had my income went wrong, then my long-term partner left me and, *mon ami*, as I said I'm not as young as I was. My health has been not good, as I have very high blood pressure and on top of everything else, my car broke down the other day and it's still in the garage. It costs such a lot to repair. It all seems to have come at once and each day is a problem but, *c'est la vie*," he smiled.

"Is there anyone back in France that can help sort things out? Have you any family?" asked Katherine.

"No, *ma chere*, they all died a long time ago. During the war, well, I feel a little awkward telling you this, but we were all in a camp, you know, my family and me and I was the only one who made it to the end of the war. I don't really understand why I was the one who was allowed to survive and not my brothers and sister. Maybe because I was young and strong when we were taken it helped me to survive. But just getting through and not knowing if you'd live to see the next day was terrible and afterwards it was always a problem for me to adapt to normal life. I had lost everything. It's all a long time ago now, but sometimes I miss them very much." Tears slowly trickled down his cheeks and he wiped them away in embarrassment.

By now, we'd eaten the pasta and I'd put some wonderful *Manchego* cheese, *pan payes* and some grapes on the table for each of us. "What do you think you'll do?" I asked him.

"Well, I could sell the house and return to France but I love my life in Ibiza and I have wonderful friends here. The island suits my nature."

"Maybe you could sell the house here and find something smaller, newer and not in need of so much work and maintenance. It wouldn't cost as much to run and it would leave you with something to live off," I suggested.

"It would be possible, it's certainly something to think about," he replied.

"I'll tell you what," Katherine suggested, "why don't we get together a bunch of friends, come up for a day, really clean up one room and paint the ceiling so that you could show it to possible buyers and in the meantime, you could always come and stay with us."

He looked down at the floor and there was a long pause. "I feel very embarrassed but yes, I would be grateful for your help. I have to say thank you. I have a spare key to the house. May I give it to you just in case I'm out when you arrive? I have an appointment with the *Notario*."

"That's settled then. It'll take us 24 hours to get everybody together. You rest and relax tomorrow, and we'll see you the following day, early in the morning."

After a coffee and another brandy, we hugged him and left Pierre smoking another Fortuna in his chair in front from the chimney. As we left, he promised to come and tell us if there was anything he needed urgently but that he'd expect us in two days time. I looked back as we went out of the front door and he was sitting there staring into the fire.

"Do you think he's OK?" I asked Katherine. "I feel bad leaving him."

"I think he should be. I left the money for today's lunch under the jar of coffee and he's got enough food and logs to last him for a couple of days."

❧

The next day, we rushed round everybody we could think of and asked them to join in helping us at Pierre's house. We ended up with about ten people who all promised to be there early in the morning.

It was a lovely day but chilly as we drove up in the direction of San Rafael. The car was laden with buckets, brushes and stepladders and as we stopped outside the house, I noticed there was no smoke coming out the chimney. I guessed Pierre had gone out to his appointment but he'd given us the key and we knew what needed doing. We were the first to arrive so I knocked on the door just in case. There was no reply and after knocking three or four times, I went round to a window that was just low enough to see in. There was no sign of him so I went back to the car and retrieved the key. Knocking on the door once more for luck and getting no reply, we opened the door and went in. "Pierre," I called out but there was no reply.

"Let's get all the gear in," Katherine suggested, "and I'll go and park the car away from the house so there's room for everyone else."

We offloaded everything and she drove away while I picked up the stepladder to take it through to the kitchen. I called out, "Pierre?" once more as I stepped through the door and immediately dropped the steps against the wall in shock. Our friend was sitting exactly where we'd left him. The fire in the chimney had gone out and the house had gone back to being cold and damp. I went over and touched his shoulder but it was clear that he had been there ever since we left and that he had died there. His cigarettes were still on the table, his last one had burned out on the edge of the ashtray, his empty glass was on the floor, as though it had fallen out of his hand and the bottle of 103 Brandy was on the table.

I heard Katherine come in with a few of our friends. There was laughter and the sound of a group of people looking forward to a busy and enjoyable day. I hurried back out to the front door. Katherine glanced at me and stopped what she was doing. "What's the matter, what is it?" she asked urgently.

"It's Pierre," I answered. I couldn't think of anything else to say.

"Is he ill?"

I explained how I had found him. "I was a nurse back in France," said Anne Marie, "let me take a look."

She came back quickly. "I'm sure it was a heart attack, and I should think it was very quick. I don't think he would have suffered. We must get the *Guardia Civil*."

ॐ

And so the authorities came and the next day an autopsy was performed. About 40 of us congregated at the church late in the afternoon on the third day for the funeral. The coffin arrived in the hearse, but having drawn up outside, the driver came over to me.

"*Señor, Vd. entiende Español, si?* Do you speak Spanish?"

I said I did. "*Gracias a dios,*" he went on. At this point, the priest came over and joined us. "What seems to be the problem" he asked quietly.

"*Señores*, it is a big problem. I have forgotten the death certificate. Can we proceed with funeral?"

"*Madre mia!*" exclaimed the priest. "How could you do such a thing? I must have the certificate! You'll have to go and get it. Quickly, before the undertaker shuts."

"But how can I?" asked the driver. "I only have the hearse."

"I'll drive you," I volunteered. And so, to the astonishment of the assembled company, we leapt into the car, and with a spinning of wheels, we shot off in the direction of Ibiza. Thankfully we were able to retrieve the missing certificate and turning round once more, we arrived in record time back at the church. With much mopping of the brow, the service and the burial was able to proceed. Happily, for those of us who didn't know the order of the service and what to do when, the church thoughtfully provided a mourner who knew the Catholic burial inside out. Obviously, she had never met Pierre but that didn't matter. We all watched her like a hawk and when she rose, the entire congregation rose and when she sat or kneeled, we followed suit. Finally, the service was over and we left the cemetery, and Pierre, and climbed into, or onto, our various cars or motorbikes and by prior agreement, we did the only sensible thing under the circumstances – we all went to a bar in Ibiza and wished Pierre *Bon Voyage*.

24.
Going Walkabout Part One

The day dawned fine and clear and at first I wondered sleepily what it was I had to do. With a jolt, I remembered and turned to tell Katherine to wake up only to find that she had put the kettle on and was having a shower. I leapt out of bed and began getting together all the things I'd need to take in a backpack for my walk. The rest of our bags would go with Katherine in the car to the port after she'd dropped me off at Antonio's. The ship would leave for Palma in the late afternoon, but I couldn't second-guess what would happen during my walk with Adelfa and I wasn't going to risk, literally, missing the boat. I'd reckoned on needing about four hours, assuming she didn't play up and everything went smoothly.

At the *finca* I put Adelfa's head collar on and with a cheerful wave from Antonio and Katherine we set off down the *camino* that eventually would lead to the outskirts of Ibiza. At first Adelfa was as good as gold, stopping occasionally to munch on a mouthful of some delicious clump of grass or some herbs that were growing beside the path. I'd wait patiently while she chewed on them meditatively and off we'd go again. A couple of hours passed and I began to think this was easy. It was then, however, that we started to pass the first houses. People sitting on the doorsteps enjoying the afternoon sun would stand up open-mouthed, peering at us. "*Hombre,*" cried a man, "*que maja, que guapa esta la yegua! Hay un circo en la ciudad?* What a beautiful horse! Is there a circus in town?"

Before I could reply, Adelfa had done a curious little dance in surprise at this stranger suddenly calling out. I stroked her neck and whispered to her but she really wasn't listening. She'd clearly decided that heading back the way we'd come was the thing to do, and with difficulty I managed to persuade her to walk past the house and to get back on course for Ibiza Town.

About now, I began to dread the moment we would arrive near the main roads. Cars, pedestrians, cyclists and people on buzzing mopeds all passing one powerful horse presented untold possibilities for disaster. And all of this was about 20 years before mobile phones. Had they existed, I could have called for reinforcements. As it was there was just me, a leading-rein and a head collar between Adelfa getting on the boat or galloping up the San Antonio road with me cantering behind.

As it was, she seemed to calm down. Maybe she was getting used to noise and sudden movements or she'd walked so far that she was feeling tired. Either way, we arrived at the entrance to the port in reasonable shape. And there, in the distance, stood Katherine next to an officer of the ferry. I could tell immediately that something had gone wrong. My spirits sank as I neared them. I'd just walked 15 kilometres and I really didn't want any bad news.

I staggered up to them and handed the leading-rein to Katherine. "What's happened?" I asked in Spanish and English.

"How do you know there's a problem?" she asked, looking at me curiously.

"Well," I replied, "call me psychic, but so far this horse and I have travelled a great many miles together and not once has anything gone smoothly. I don't know what it is but I just saw the way you were standing and the look on your face and I got this feeling that something wasn't going to work out."

"Oh dear," Katherine murmured sadly, "I don't know how to tell you this."

"I knew it," I growled in Spanish, glaring at the ship's officer. "I bloody knew it. I don't suppose there's an albatross around anywhere is there? Maybe there's one on the boat."

"Sssh," Katherine reprimanded me, "you'll upset Adelfa if you shout."

"*Que ha pasado*? What's happened?" I demanded, staring at them both.

"*Señor,*" stammered the sailor, "*Por favor, calmense,* please be calm*, hay un problema pequeño, si, pero no es culpa mio,* it's the engine of the ship, she is not working and the ship she doesn't go, we do not go to Palma de Mallorca this day."

Katherine told me later that my reaction was like that of a small volcano erupting. "I'm cursed," I cried in Spanish. "I've just walked 15 kilometres, I'm tired, my feet hurt, I have a horse that is worth a great deal of money who is also tired and thirsty and you tell me that there is a small problem. I'll tell you about this problem. I'm going to have to walk another 15 kilometres back to Antonio's *finca,* then I'm going to have go home and get up very early tomorrow morning, go to the wonderful *Telefonica* and try and stop our friend Lisa, *una señora Americana,* driving all the way to Palma with a horse box attached to the back of her car. Then I am going to have to go back to our friend Antonio and explain why there is a horse in his stable once more. Then I'm going to have to re-book my *yegua, la Señora* and me on your blasted boat once again. And *Señor*, you tell me I have *un problema pequeño.* Will you walk back to the *finca* with me tonight?"

And then, of course, the ship's officer did something that made me feel a complete heel and which deflated me completely. Adelfa was chewing delicately on the gold braid on his shoulder and he was so upset over the whole situation, especially with me getting so angry, that a single tear trickled slowly down his cheek. "Oh *señor, estoy muy triste,* I am so sad that this beautiful horse is so tired, that you have so many *problemas. Que puedo decir?* I look forward to welcoming you on board our ship on the next possible voyage to Palma."

Katherine looked at me worriedly. "Will you be OK to do the walk again? Do you want me to leave the car here and go with you?"

"No, it's OK," I sighed reassuring her. "I'm only concerned for Adelfa. I need a bucket of water for her and some feed. Then we'll wait for an hour and set off once more."

A bucket of water was produced by round-eyed sailors from the ferry who stared at my little Adelfa as she munched on some alfalfa that we had brought in the car for the boat trip. However, I knew that if we waited too long both of us would start to stiffen up and so once more we began the long trip back to Antonio's farm.

I'm not sure who was wearier as we crawled back up the 15 kilometres of the *camino*. The moon had come up behind the hills and still Adelfa and I trudged on. I began to wonder if we were part of some ancient Greek legend of a man and a horse condemned to wander for all eternity and never reach a satisfactory destination. Gone was Adelfa's friskiness of the outward journey and I think she must have thought she was destined to spend the rest of her life taking part in mammoth walks with me. We got back to Antonio's farm in the early hours of the morning and I quietly bedded down my beloved horse.

The house was totally silent and I crept up the *camino* in the direction of the main road that led in the direction of Santa Gertrudis. I was desperately hoping for someone to come past who'd give me a lift. If there were no cars at that time of night, I decided to sleep by the side of the road. But there, facing in the direction of home was our car with Katherine asleep in the driver's seat. I knocked on the window and she opened her eyes. "Evening sailor," she grinned seductively, "fancy a lift home?"

"You don't begin to know how much!" I started to laugh as I climbed into the passenger seat. "I think I've had enough for one day."

25.
All the Nice Gulls...

The next morning I could barely walk. My legs ached more than I could believe possible and to my surprise they became incredibly bruised over the next few days. It was with difficulty that I went to see Antonio. I climbed out of the car almost doubled up with stiffness. "*Hombre,*" he roared with laughter, "*parece como un viejo,* you look like an old man. Haven't you lived in Ibiza long enough to know that things can go wrong sometimes? *Estoy muy contento que la yegua ha vuelto en casa* – I'm really happy that she has come home again. All you have to do now is to book another passage to Palma de Mallorca and then take another *paseo* with Adelfa. After all, it's only 15 kilometres to Ibiza," he grinned clapping me on the back. "But first, come inside and have a *carajillo.* It will make a new man of you."

As we walked towards the front of his *finca*, I paused and glanced up. It was such a beautiful home that I couldn't visit it without stopping and admiring the textures formed by the layers of white cal that had been painted on the walls over the years and the use of wooden beams to support much of the roof. These had gone that extraordinary grey colour that only comes with weathering over many years and above the entrance was a balcony that at the right time of the year was used for drying almonds. Hanging up to dry were strings of figs and I knew from previous visits that there might well be a heap of corn.

Once it had dried, the *maiz,* the corn was ready to cook. Antonio would sit in the deep shade with a glass of local wine, take the kernels off the cob by twisting it through his hands and then go downstairs to make popcorn. First he'd light the hob of the *butano* gas stove and then he'd take a large, flat old frying pan into which he'd pour a quantity of olive oil. He'd add some salt and then heat the oil till it smoked.

The incredible scent of hot olive oil would fill the air as he deftly dropped in the corn. Then he'd cover the pan with a heavy sheet of tin and give it a careful shake. While we'd wait for what sounded gunfire to erupt from within the pan, he'd put out a dish of olives, perhaps a plate of cheese and *jamon Serrano*, some *pan payes* and another bottle of red wine. As soon as the explosions from within the pan had ceased, he'd empty the popcorn into a large bowl, sprinkle some more salt over it, give it a shake, put the whole lot on a tray and we'd carry it outside to the porch where we'd sit and pass the time of day. Time in Ibiza seemed longer than anywhere else and with a good companion, the silences were better than the conversation. Inevitably, once we'd sorted out the world and anything else that came to mind, we'd wander over to Adelfa's stable and continue our conversation with her. She'd amble over and place her silken muzzle on the top of her stable door within easy reach for a convenient human hand to stroke her. Her large, liquid eyes would peer happily at her humans. Eventually, she'd make that happy, throaty sort of noise that only a horse makes that has been exercised, fed, watered and caressed.

On this particular day I hobbled painfully into the living room. An electric light hung down from the wonderful *sabina* pine beams that supported the floor above. In the corner stood a large fridge and parked neatly against the back wall was Antonio's gleaming new motorbike. I went over and admired it. "Antonio," I asked him, "*Sabia que tiene una Yamaha nueva pero que potencia tiene?* How many cc is it?"

He laughed and came over to stroke the machine. "*Mas que la yegua, amigo mio.* More than your horse! *Y dime*, tell me about your expedition to *la ciudad*, the city, with Adelfa. What happened?" Then he busied himself about the kitchen putting together an array of dishes, glasses and bottles that clearly he felt were necessary for a snack to keep body and soul together.

I explained about the fiasco of the previous evening and apologised for having to bring my little mare back to her stable. "*Por favor, hombre*" exclaimed Antonio, "don't you realise that it gives me a great deal of pleasure having her here with me. But, seriously, will you try again to take her to Palma de Mallorca?"

"Yes," I answered, "we're going to do the whole thing again next week but I need a few days to let my legs recover."

"You know your *problema*? *Solamente tiene dos piernas*. You only have two legs, Adelfa has four so she will recover far quicker," he giggled as he went into the popcorn-making routine. "Café or *vino*? And please go and sit. You are very tired and you should rest."

"Could I have a very strong coffee? If I had a glass of wine this morning, I'd be asleep in five minutes?"

"*Ningun problema*," he replied. "And the *señora Americana* in Mallorca – is she able to make the arrangements again for next week? I could always come with you if you want."

"*Querido amigo,* my dear friend, I wouldn't dream of such a thing. I can't believe that there'll be the same problem two weeks running. And besides, I've spoken to *nuestra amiga* Lisa, and she's going to come over on the previous boat from Palma to meet us with her car and trailer so that we can put Adelfa in it for the journey. That should make all the difference. And also she has much more experience than I do with moving horses around, so I'm feeling much better about the whole expedition."

"*Estoy muy contento*," exclaimed Antonio. "My concern is that you arrive safely in Pollensa and that Adelfa *esta enamorada con su nuevo marido*, is pleased with her husband."

The week seemed to be flying past and gradually the stiffness left my back and legs and I started to manage to walk upright once more. Katherine stopped pointing out how much like a chimp my posture had become and generally I felt more like a human again. It was September, the sea had retained the heat from the summer, and we had a couple of days relaxing on the rocks at Es Pou d'es Llou. We took a grill with us, plus a frying pan, some bacon, eggs, mushrooms and tomatoes, a large bunch of grapes, a fresh loaf of *pan payes*, a box of matches and a couple of bottles of white wine. When we arrived at the water's edge, Katherine put the bottles in a net bag and tethered them in a pool to keep cool while I gathered some kindling and firewood, plus some pine twigs for starting the fire. Ibiza has an abundance of wild herbs such as thyme and rosemary and we collected some to put on the fire.

Before cooking the food, we swam out a couple of hundred yards and looked back at the rocks and further round at the beach. As always, this was one of the most enchanting bays anywhere around the coast of Ibiza. The dark velvet sea was like a balm to my muscles and as we headed back to the rocks I felt my optimism for the journey to Mallorca growing.

If they're dry enough, pine twigs can be lit simply with a match and it wasn't long before the fire was hot enough to get on with the cooking. Because we were some distance from the nearest trees and the fire was on bare rock next to the sea, I didn't have to worry about the chance of starting a forest fire.

The next step was to put the *pan payes*, the loaf of bread, alongside the frying pan on the grill and place some of the herbs on the flames. They gave the bread the most incredible aromatic, smoky, toasted flavour and it wasn't long before we cut the loaf lengthways, sprinkled on some olive oil and salt and then made delicious *bocadillos*, sandwiches, that were filled with the bacon and fried eggs. As the oil ran down our hands we settled down to enjoy our meal. We shared the tomatoes and mushrooms straight from the pan and the white wine helped the day to mellow and us to become relaxed and at ease with the next stage of the Adelfa adventure.

❧

As the afternoon wore on, I remembered the time just before my first walk to Ibiza with Adelfa when we'd decided to spend the day at the beach. Coming down to the rocks we neared the place where you could climb down to the flat rocks. We heard a raucous cawing, screeching noise that sounded like an animal in pain. Sure enough, as we looked over the edge, we saw a seagull with what looked like a broken wing and it seemed as if it was trapped between two rocks. I tried to get near him but his beak looked razor sharp and he was in no mood to let me deal with him. Cowardice seemed the best option so we went to the car and drove back in the direction of the pension.

There was a *campesino,* a farmer, walking down the *camino* so I stopped the car and asked him if he knew where we could get help for the gull.

"*Caray, Señor, este tipo de pajaro esta muy peligroso* – this is a dangerous bird and you must be very careful. There is a *pescador*, a fisherman who lives in a *finca* back in the direction of Playa Es Figueral who might be able to do something. He understands the way of birds and they seem to respond to him. If you can find him at home, he will certainly come back with you. Here is how you find him," and on a scrap of paper I found in the car he drew a map. "His name is Pep – tell him that I sent you."

We piled back into the car and headed off to find Pep the fisherman. Fortunately, he turned out to be at home. His house was small and it looked as though it had been there forever. Pep was equally small, his clothes were worn, his face weather beaten and physically he looked as though life had been a struggle. But as we explained what we'd found, a spark came into his eyes as though he looked forward to the challenge of saving the seagull. Fortunately, he agreed to come back with us. He also made two requests. "*El primero, Señor*, the first thing is that if we can catch this *pajero*, you must agree to bring us back to my *finca*. He will be too big for me to carry and anyway it would take too long. The second is, if there is nothing to be done, I shall need your help to kill him. We cannot leave a wounded animal to die a painful death." I agreed to the first without a problem. I didn't look forward to the second but I couldn't exactly chicken out and so I said I'd do my best to help. Privately, I couldn't think of a single thing I could do that would be of any help whatsoever.

Pep gathered up a couple of sacks, a large *cesta,* a round, flat basket with a couple of handles, a short piece of thin rope, a stout stick, a large white cloth and what looked like a long bandage. Putting all of this into the boot of the car, we went back to Es Pou d'es Llou as quickly as possible. As we approached the edge of the rocks, the angry gull was yelling his head off every bit as much as before. Pep peered down at him, summing up the situation. "*Menos mal que el pajaro esta atrapado* – good thing the bird is trapped – it makes things a bit easier. But we must be very careful that he is not hurt anymore."

Proving to be remarkably agile, he climbed down and I passed him all the various things we'd brought with us. The gull leant forward, opened his beak and yammered his anger, pain and frustration at us. Pep indicated to Katherine that she should stay well clear as he prepared to attempt the rescue. "*Usted,* you," he indicated to me, "You stand here in front of him with this stick. Attract his attention while I go behind him with this sack. Hold the stick towards him and as he goes for it, I will try and drop the sack over his head."

"Is his wing broken?" Katherine asked nervously.

"*Si, Señorita,* it is certainly broken but first we must make him calm by making everything dark for him, before we can judge how bad the break is." As he said this, Pep edged his way round behind the rocks that held the gull fast. The bird tried to see where his potential enemy was going but I did my best to carry out Pep's instructions by distracting the gull. He lunged forward at the stick, cursing and swearing at the top of his voice. I lurched backwards at the same moment that Pep moved forward and dropped the sack neatly over the bird's head. "*Rapido,*" he cried, "get the rope and tie the sack loosely round his neck."

Despite the bird having calmed down considerably once he found himself in the dark, I approached him with some caution. Once the sack was tied he had pretty much given up the fight and Pep was able to examine the broken wing. His gnarled hands were gentle as he worked the feathers back to allow him to see the extent of the damage. "*Pobrecito*," he muttered, "poor thing, he must have been in some pain. But, *menos mal,* it is a clean break. Come and look." I leant over the rock and realised the broken bone had penetrated the skin on the bird's wing. "Can you heal it?" I asked.

"I'll do my best," he replied. "Fetch me the bandage and we'll make the wing safe."

He took the thin strip of material and by feeling down the gull's side, he passed the bandage round and round its body until he had both the broken and the good wing fastened against its sides. "Now bring the *cesta* over here and help me to lift him out of the rocks and onto the basket. We'll bring the sides up round him and tie the handles together."

The second the bird felt himself being lifted up, he started to struggle again, his legs paddling like crazy, but by now most of the fight had gone out of him. Between us we managed to place him on the basket and to do as Pep had directed. So now the only thing left was to find a way of carrying the gull up the steep rocks and over to the car.

Once we'd achieved that, we placed him carefully in the boot of the car where the gull lay muttering dark thoughts to himself about what he'd do to us once he was free while I drove us quickly back to Pep's home. There he transferred the gull to a box with a chicken wire front in which he'd previously kept rabbits. "Isn't it too small for such a large bird?" asked Katherine.

"No, no, *Señorita,* he must be kept calm for a while. Then I will examine the wing and make splints for above and below the break so that the wound is kept secure. He will be quite safe as he is but he is going to have stay in the box so that he cannot move around and take off the bandage."

As we weren't leaving for Mallorca for another four days, I asked if we could come back in a couple of days to find out how the bird was getting on. "*Naturalmente, Señor*. It will be my pleasure and I will wait for you to come at any time in the morning. I am grateful for all your help."

Two days later, we drove down the *camino* to Pep's house. I'd brought with me a bottle of the best Mari Mayans Hierbas that money could buy as a thank you to him for all he'd done for the gull. As we walked towards the front door, Pep appeared from the large shed next to the main house. "*Buenos dias, Señores*, good morning," he smiled. "I am very glad you could come to see how my new *animalito* is getting on. Please come with me." He turned and led us in to the shed. An irritable squawk came from the box but in some strange way, it no longer sounded full of pain.

Pep had removed the sack from the bird's head but the gull's body was still held in the box. "He's eating again, *Señor*. I went out in my boat yesterday afternoon and he is enjoying some of the fish I caught. I think we are over the worst now and I'll keep him in the box some while. Then, when I feel the break has healed, I shall let him out within the *almacen*, the shed, for a while until he builds up his strength again. When he is strong enough to go back out into the world, I shall send a message to you to come and see him fly."

The bird's eye had been following us as we talked. From time to time, he'd let out a cry of 'yarp, yarp' and rustle his feathers inside the box. But, thank heavens, the dreadful sound of terror was no longer present.

As we went back outside, I remembered the bottle on the back seat of the car. Handing it to Pep, we both expressed our gratitude to him for rescuing the gull and for his continuing care. He looked at the bottle and back at us. "*Señores*," he said, "I would be honoured if you would have the first drink of Hierbas from this wonderful gift. Please come and sit down and I will get glasses."

He disappeared inside for a few moments and came back out with three small tumblers. He carefully poured three drinks and raised his glass in a toast. "*Salud a Ustedes, y al pajaro en el almacen*. I wish you both good health and also to the gull." He then explained that he had been a widower for some years and his real pleasure in life now came from looking after animals that needed help. "They are very often unable to help themselves and it is the least we can do for the little ones."

He told us how often animals found themselves in terrible situations when they were completely helpless. Pep recalled going out fishing one day and finding another gull floating helplessly on the water with fishing line tangled round its legs. "It was very close to the end and had I not been lucky enough to find it, the poor creature would have starved and drowned. Of course, catching it wasn't as easy as the other day but it was quite weak and I managed." I looked at him and imagined the hardships of his life, how he had coped since his wife died and what an amazingly gentle man he was.

I told him about Adelfa and the journey we were going to be making in a couple of days. I also related briefly the story of my epic journey with her across Spain. Again that look came in his eyes at the mention of an animal. "*Caray*, I'd love to see the *yegua, Señor*, she must be very beautiful."

"Would you like to meet her before she goes to Mallorca?" I asked. "I'm sure Antonio wouldn't mind if we took you to his *finca*."

"But I have never been to *la ciudad de Ibiza*," he replied nervously. "I've never seen Ibiza town. How would I travel there to see the *yegua*?"

"We'd take you there and bring you home again – it wouldn't take long."

It was plain he was wrestling with the idea but then he said quietly, "I think it would be better if you could describe the horse to me and I shall paint a picture of her in my mind. She sounds very beautiful – tell me about her again, please – and where she came from."

And so I described my little mare with care and in detail. Pep had trouble understanding the concept of an Arab mare at first but he came to understand the practicality of the breed when I told him that their nostrils expand when they are galloping in the desert. This allows them to breathe more easily and that's why they have become known as 'Drinkers of the Wind'.

I told him about my journey to Ibiza with Adelfa and how she was going to Mallorca to meet her *marido*, her husband, because we wanted to breed Arab horses. "*Madre dios*," he murmured, "imagine what a wonderful thing it would be to have this in Ibiza."

"Can I ask you something?" I queried.

"Of course, anything," he smiled.

"Are you a…" and here I paused because I wasn't sure of the word. "I think the word is *curandero*, a healer of animals."

"Some say I am," he replied softly. "I have always had a love of the little ones and I am lucky that they have always responded to me. I do not cure them but they let me help them."

"And is it the same with *la gente*, with people?" Katherine asked.

"*Ah Señora*, that is the question. With the people the mind gets in the way, and also some people cannot trust you in the same way that an animal can. I could not help my *Señora* either." He sighed deeply. "But that is many years ago and now I have a friend in the almacen who needs my help, so I am grateful to you, *Señores*. And you have told me about *la yegua* and this have given me much to think about."

As we left Pep, I asked if it would be all right if we came back on our return from Mallorca to see how the bird was progressing.

Pep nodded happily. "I shall look forward to your return," he said and as we drove off, he stood outside his *finca* waving goodbye and I knew the gull couldn't be in better hands.

26.
Going Walkabout Part Two

The day arrived for me to collect Adelfa and set off for the port once again. Katherine dropped me off at the *finca* and as Antonio was nowhere to be seen, I put her head collar on. The little horse gave a contented sigh. Clearly she thought we were going outside for a gentle stroll and maybe some lunging but once we arrived at the point where we left Antonio's land, she gave me a dirty look and skipped sideways nervously as much to say, "Are you crazy? We're not going through all that again are we?"

"Oh no," I said sternly as I turned to face her. I pulled her head round so that I looked her straight in the eye. "I don't want to do this walk any more than you do, but we're going to do it together and we're going off to Mallorca together, so you might as well do it with good grace. Now come on, let's go."

I turned round and found Antonio had come up behind me and was laughing his head off. "*Hombre,*" he giggled, "*entiende Ingles la Adelfa*? Does she speak English?"

"*Que haces acqui?* What are you doing here?" I asked him.

"Oh well, it seemed like a good day for a *paseo*, a stroll into Ibiza so I decided I'd keep you company," he grinned. "A friend will drop me home afterwards. I wouldn't want to end up looking like you did after the last time. Oh, and by the way, I thought we might need this," he grinned, pulling a bottle of cognac from one pocket and two glasses from another.

I laughed and turned back to Adelfa. "*Que te parece, chica? Es un buen amigo, no?* What do you think? He's a good friend, isn't he?" I asked her. Adelfa gave a soft whinny and ambled towards Antonio who took an apple from his pocket, cut it in half with a penknife and gave it to her. My little Arab, being a sucker for a bribe, munched happily on it as Antonio took the leading-rein from me and set off down the *camino*. We chatted as we walked towards the island's capital and the journey seemed to pass in half the time it had taken the previous week. Of course, maybe the brandy helped as we stopped for a drink after half an hour.

Antonio asked me about life in England, what it was like being an actor and whether I thought I'd stay on in Ibiza. I explained that for me, home was now in Ibiza for the foreseeable future and yet, while I'd been an actor that had seemed the only life possible.

I tried as best as I could to tell him what weekly repertory theatre was like and how, once upon a time, I'd spent six months in Folkestone doing not just weekly rep, but a matinee and an evening performance every day. On Sunday afternoons you'd do the dress rehearsal, on the Monday morning you'd do a final run-through and then, at 2.30pm, the curtain would rise on that week's play. In the meantime, you'd be desperately busy trying to forget the lines from the previous week's show.

"It meant working from 9am until 11pm for six days of every week and then going home and learning the lines," I explained.

"*No entiendo como Vd. podria aprender tantos palabras,*" said Antonio, shaking his head "How can you learn so much week after week?"

"With a lot of difficulty," I laughed. "Somehow, though, the more you learned, the more you could learn. I remember one time when I was in a show on tour and I was playing second lead. At the same time I was understudying the leading man and because of the build up to the first night, it meant I hadn't really had time to learn his part. After about two weeks on the road, the leading man developed laryngitis and I had to take over. Partly because I'd heard him throughout the rehearsals and also because I'd had that time in weekly rep learning script after script, I managed to learn 75 per cent of the part during the night and the next day. That night I went on and with a bit of ad libbing and help from the other actors, I managed to get through it."

"*Dios mio*, I could never do such a thing. I would have an *infarto,* a heart attack. And what did you do on television?"

"The first time, I was in a series about the police."

"*Caray*, were you a policeman?"

"No, no, I committed a murder that time."

Antonio started to giggle and then he laughed almost until he cried. "*Amigo mio*," he said as his laughter turned into a coughing fit, "I cannot imagine you as an *asesino*. You just don't look like one. How could you possibly act the part if you have never done a murder?"

As we walked along, I tried to explain how an actor works into the part so that whatever you are playing, you make it believable to the audience.

"But then, if you are *completamente* believing that you are an *assasino,* why did you not actually kill the other actors?"

It was hard to describe the ability of an actor to be the character and yet to maintain his or her normal control over the immediate surroundings and the relationships with the other performers. I was once in a production of *Great Expectations* by the great English writer, Charles Dickens. I was playing the part of the grown-up Pip and I came on for the first time in the second act. As I walked to the door to make my first entrance, I found what was supposed to be my front door had stuck and I couldn't go on stage. Other members of the cast were waiting on stage for me to appear and were wondering what was happening. The only way I could go on was to open a window in the set and climb through that, to the great surprise of the audience and the cast. The problem that presented itself was that every time anyone had to enter or exit during that Act, they had to climb in and out of the window. As you can imagine, it wasn't easy retaining control of the situation. That's what I mean by being 'in the part' but also managing to continue with the circumstances you're in.

Antonio's eyes were round and he was biting his lip in an attempt to stop himself laughing. "You went on to the stage through a window?" he chortled. "*Hombre, que profesion mas increible*, what an extraordinary business it is being an actor. Imagine in real life entering your home through the window."

☙

At this moment, two things happened. Adelfa stopped dead as she decided to graze on some tasty looking grass growing in the shade of an algarrobo tree at the side of the *camino*. At the same time, coming towards us was the first person we'd seen since we set out. It was an elderly Ibicenco on a moped. He slowed down by placing both his feet flat on the ground. The effect was rather like throwing an anchor over the side of a dinghy and as he neared us, he managed to skid to halt, nearly toppling over the handlebars. Taking off his black beret, the new arrival scratched his scalp, replaced the beret, stared owlishly at Adelfa and back at us and then back at the mare. During this time he wobbled from side to side, looking very much the worse for the wear. "*Hola, Señores, no quisiero molestar la yegua*, I don't want to upset the mare with the noise of the Mobyllette. Could I ask what *raza* she is? I have never before seen a horse that was so beautiful – she is not unlike my *esposa* – my wife. The horse must be very rare," he slurred.

I handed the leading-rein to Antonio and went over to shake the old man's hand. "*Buenos tardes, Señor*. Thank you for thinking about the noise of the Mobyllette. She is a purebred Arab and I am taking her to Mallorca to stables where there is a wonderful stallion. I want to breed Arab horses."

"She is very noble. Have you ridden her?" he asked, an aura of alcohol enveloping me as he spoke.

"No," I replied, "she's only three years old and I'll ride her later on. We're on our way to catch the ferry to Palma this evening."

The old man asked, "May I talk to her?"

"Of course," I said, "let me hold your *moto*."

After several attempts, he dismounted with some difficulty and tottered over to Adelfa, shaking Antonio's hand as he did so.

The mare stopped munching and looked up at him. She let out a whinny of pleasure and immediately pushed her muzzle under his jacket. Antonio laughed. "What have you got in your pocket, *Señor?*" he asked.

"*Ay, madre mia,*" confided the old man placing one finger carefully alongside his nose, "*tengo un paquete de mentas.* I have a packet of mints to suck so that my wife doesn't know that sometimes I have a drink or two. What a clever horse! May I offer one to her?"

Antonio looked over at me and I answered, "As long as they are not too strong. She loves mints and would eat the whole packet."

The old man reached into his inner jacket pocket and pulled out the mints. Little Adelfa promptly did a small dance of expectation and let out several squeaks that mingled hope and frustration that she couldn't get at them at once. Clearly she was worried that the wretched humans might be greedy and not share them with her. Strong as he was, Antonio was tugged back and forth like a dinghy behind a large yacht.

"*Me llamo Paco, Señores,*" said our newfound friend politely as he wavered slightly. "My name is Paco." As he spoke, he turned round to look at me, trod on a stone, lost his footing and promptly fell over backwards. The bag of mints flew out of his hand and several were scattered on the *camino*. Adelfa's head shot downwards and she managed to scoop up at least three before Antonio, tugging manfully on the reins, managed to pull her head up. A dreamy look came into her eyes as she crunched her way through the sweets. Collecting Paco off the ground where he lay like a stranded beetle on his back, I gathered what remained of his mints and led him over to his *moto*. "It might be better if you went on home," I suggested to him.

"But I could come with you to the port and help you *with La Señorita Adelfa,*" he giggled archly, putting his head on one side. "She likes me, I believe, and maybe she wants me to come to Palma de Mallorca with you. I've never been there, and it would be something to tell my *esposa* when I came back." I pointed out that this was impossible as there were only two tickets available.

Time was getting on and I could see Antonio signalling to me by making revving gesture with his hands that I should help the old man onto his *moto* and send him on his way. Also, I could just begin to detect Paco's good humour changing to truculence as he stared belligerently around him. "*Quien ha robado mi maquina*? Who has stolen my machine?"

"It's here," I answered, indicating that I was holding it ready for him to climb aboard. In the meantime, Antonio had moved quietly round Paco with Adelfa in tow and was walking off down the lane in the direction of the port. "On you get," I said with a definite degree of false heartiness, as I manhandled him onto his Mobyllette. "I don't think I want to go home," grumbled Paco from the depths of the several large drinks he'd had earlier, "I want to come with you to Menorca."

"We aren't going to Menorca, we're off to Palma." Suddenly inspiration struck. "I tell you what, I'll go to your *casa* and tell your *Señora* how we spent several hours having drinks together and how you've decided you don't want to go home and that you're coming to Palma."

His reaction was really odd. It was like watching the air coming out of a balloon as the irritability escaped from Paco at high speed. Somehow, he'd miraculously sobered up. "Ooh, *Señor*," he cried nervously clutching at my arm and massaging the sleeve of my jacket. "*Oh no, Señor, no, no, no, por favor, ay Dios mio, que me voy hacer? No debes decir tal cosa a mi esposa, por favor no!* Please, please don't go and tell my wife any such thing. *Sabes, ella esta una angelita,*" he babbled, pedalling frantically at the *maquina* until the motor erupted into life. "She is an angel but just occasionally when she thinks I might have had anything to do with alcoholic drinks, which

I never do, of course, she becomes slightly less of an angel." Popping a mint into his mouth he handed me the packet. "Here, *Señor*, take these as a *regalo*, a gift for the *yegua. Bon viatje, Señor*." With that he took off up the *camino* as though he'd been shot from a cannon.

27.

A Train to Barcelona

Hurrying off down the lane, it took me about five minutes to catch up with Antonio and his charge who seemed to be behaving remarkably well under his firm hand. "*Hola*," he grinned, "how did you manage to persuade our friend that he wasn't wanted on the voyage?"

I explained how I'd offered to help Paco by talking to his wife about his wish to join us on the trip to Mallorca. Antonio started to laugh so much that finally he had to stop and hold onto Adelfa. "*Ay de mi*, that is the most terrible threat you could make. His life would have been impossible if you had done such a thing and then he really would have had to move to Mallorca."

And so we continued until Ibiza town came into sight. Having the two of us in charge certainly made me feel more optimistic. Our feelings seemed to be transmitted to the little mare who gazed calmly round as we trudged through the back streets towards the port. I realised that one of the things I really loved about the Spanish was the fact that two men could walk through the streets of a busy town with a pretty spectacular looking horse in tow and nobody treated it as anything strange.

One or two people emerged from bars and shops but all they did was to murmur praise for Adelfa. "*Que bonita, la yegua,*" said one. "*Ay Señores, que preciosa, esta como una angelita. Mira, hija,*" said a woman holding the hand of her daughter and pointing at Adelfa, "*¡Esta tan maja, la yegua!* Look, darling, the horse is so beautiful!" It may have been tiredness but I suddenly got the feeling that I could have walked through the streets on my hands and I might have received some applause or polite comments, but nothing else.

❧

Spaniards may be curious about what you are doing but on the whole, as long as you aren't harming anyone, there's a kind of dignity in how they deal with you. I think they assume that you probably know best and you're left to get on with your own business. Only once have I seen real anger in a large group of Spaniards. I was in a bar late one afternoon, chatting with someone I knew when suddenly the bar started to empty and the men of the village gathered in the Plaza.

Following them outside, I asked a local that I knew what was happening. He explained that a 12-year old schoolgirl had been attacked on her way home. She'd been grabbed by a man who tried to drag her into a shed. Fortunately, she managed to wriggle free before anything worse happened and ran home sobbing and in a bad state. Word had jumped from mouth to mouth like a forest fire and that was why the men were standing in the Plaza. There was such an ominous silence that I asked what they would do next. My friend answered me, "*Señor*, we do not allow this kind of thing to happen in Spain. This man, we know who he is and he had better hope that the *Guardia Civil* catch him before we do otherwise…"

What they would actually have done, I don't know… but as a race, the Spanish won't tolerate anyone who harms a child and I wouldn't have placed a bent penny on the perpetrator walking away unharmed if they'd found him. As it turned out, he was caught pretty quickly and smuggled away by boat by the *Guardia* to stand trial elsewhere.

As we entered the port area I spotted Katharine in the distance and standing next to her was Lisa with her horsebox parked nearby. They were both waving cheerfully and my heart lifted at the thought that this time we were actually going to get on the boat. Antonio handed the leading-rein to me and shook hands with Lisa. "*Buenos tardes, Señoritas, finalmente hemos llegado*, finally we've arrived. I don't know how Adelfa is feeling but me,

I need *una cerveza*." With that he strode off in the direction of a small bar where he was clearly well known and promptly returned with four bottles of San Miguel. He then did what I'd only ever seen done once before and that was to hook the metal cap on his lower teeth, close his upper teeth on the cap and with a quick twist of the wrist, the cap came off.

Both Lisa and Katharine let out squeals of dismay and cries of, "Oh no, don't do that – stop, stop, you're bad!!"

Antonio's grin stretched from ear to ear as he took a bottle opener out of his pocket and showed it to them. "*Mira Señoritas*, I loosened it first with this. But," he continued, "I have a friend who can do it for real. He doesn't loosen it but I don't like the *dentistas* enough to try it properly."

Katharine went over and pretended to punch him on the chest with both fists. "You're a bad boy, Antonio. Don't scare me like that again," she scolded him.

In the meantime, Adelfa was looking round her. She'd spotted the horsebox which obviously carried the smell of other horses that had travelled in it. She tugged gently on the leading-rein and I strolled along beside her. The ramp at the back was down and peering inside, she marched firmly up and into the box. We all looked in amazement at each other until Lisa pointed out that there was tasty net of hay inside. "No, no, *Señorita* Lisa, she is anxious to get on with the journey and to meet her new *marido*, her husband," laughed Antonio.

As we were going to have to load onto the roll on/roll off ferry in about an hour's time, we decided to leave her inside and Lisa quietly raised the ramp so that Adelfa was safely inside. "One more *cerveza* to celebrate, *mis amigos*?" asked Antonio. "After all, I have to return the *abretapas*, the bottle opener?" We all agreed and off he went again.

I was standing there quietly looking at Adelfa when an Englishman, his downtrodden-looking wife and a bored daughter in tow, came marching down the harbour. Eyeing me up and down, he barked, "You English?" I was instantly tempted to say no, I was Spanish, but I guess I was caught off guard for a moment.

"Er… yes. Can I help you?"

"Probably more than the locals," he said rudely. "We're looking for the train station but I can't seem to make any of these wretched people understand me. We want to catch the last train to Barcelona. Some friends have arrived there," he said importantly, "and they want us to join them."

"But there aren't any trains," I replied, somewhat startled. "You're on an island."

"What do you mean, we're on an island? Did you hear that," he shouted turning to his wife, "bloody fool says we're on an island."

The wife looked worried. "On an island, dear? Didn't you check before we left?" The daughter muttered, "Mum, I don't want to be on an island."

"We can't be on an island," growled the husband, obviously annoyed that his wife should think him to be anything less than perfect. "What the devil do you mean? You're as bad as the rest of them."

By this time, Antonio had returned with another four beers. He looked at Katharine and Lisa. Katharine translated, "This man wants to catch the train to Barcelona and he can't seem to understand why there isn't one."

"*No me diga,* don't tell me!" he replied trying his best not to explode with laughter.

I was beginning to be slightly irritated. "The fact is," I said, turning back to the family, "Ibiza is an island, it has been for thousands of years and there are no trains. For heaven's sake, how on earth did you get here?"

The husband began to make volcano-erupting noises about people who drank too many beers in the sun and who didn't know what they were talking about. His wife interrupted him. "Well, we went to the travel agent and said we wanted somewhere near the sea that was guaranteed to be warm. She told us that Ibiza would suit us nicely. She did say it was quite near Barcelona. Are we really on an island? You know, surrounded by water?" she queried tremulously.

"Yes, you really are, I'm afraid and you are quite close to Barcelona but there's a lot of sea in between." Suddenly I had a thought. "What time did your plane take off?"

"About 2am," growled the husband. "Why?"

"So you took off in the dark and landed in the dark?"

"Yes, so what?"

"You never saw that you were crossing the Mediterranean and landing on an island? And your travel agent never mentioned it?"

"Well I never," said the wife. "Fancy that!"

At this point, little Adelfa gave a kick of boredom on the back door of the box. She'd been ignored by what she regarded as her family for long enough and was making herself heard.

"What was that?" asked the daughter nervously.

"It's our horse," I told her, "We're taking her to Mallorca."

"By train?" asked the little girl hopefully. "We're going on a train?"

"For goodness sake, do be quiet," snapped her father. He turned to me. "Looks to me as though you're being cruel to that horse, keeping her shut up in that horrible little box. I've a good mind to report you to the local RSPCA."

"Oh, come along dear," sighed his wife. "It's nothing to do with us." She turned and trudged back up the port with her husband blustering and puffing after her.

I translated the entire conversation to Antonio who was overcome with hysterical laughter and had to sit down on a bollard to recover. "*Dios mio,* I have to tell my friends this. Is it supposed to be an underwater train?" he gurgled happily and

I knew that within a day, dozens of people would be chuckling over the idea of a train to Barcelona.

Finally we were loaded onto the roll on/roll off ferry, made sure Adelfa was safe and secure and the three of us went up on deck to wave goodbye to Antonio. He was standing with a group of friends who were mopping tears of laughter from their eyes. I could guess exactly what they were being told and it was having the effect I'd predicted. One of them glanced up and saw us looking down at them. He nudged Antonio who in turn saw us and promptly started to make railway engine hooting and 'chuff, chuff, chuff' noises. The small group collapsed against each other again until one of them headed off to the bar and came back with yet more beers.

As the crew started to haul up the passenger's gangplank, I called down, "*Vamos a ver la yegua, veremos pronto,* we're going to go down and look after Adelfa. See you soon." And at that moment, after all the laughter, I saw Antonio, his face suddenly looking serious, appear a little lost, as though he'd suddenly been given the bad news that we were actually going. I was in no doubt that it was the horse he was going to miss the most but in my turn I felt that sadness I always had when I was leaving Ibiza, a real tug that I, along with everyone who had been privileged to live there, felt when they departed. It was silly, I guess, given that we were only going for a short while and that Ibiza was at most four hours away by ferry from Mallorca, but there you are, that's how powerful the pull of a place can be.

I remembered a particularly wise English woman I met in Ibiza briefly. She said to me, "Ibiza draws you in when she wants to, and she sends you on your way when the time is right." I never felt that was truer than when I was standing on the deck watching the port of Ibiza receding as the propeller chewed up the water and pushed us on our way.

The voyage across was uneventful with Adelfa proving just how seasoned a sailor she had become. Gone were the days of trying to kick her way out of a travelling box. Of course, it could have been that she was tired from marching up and down the *camino* but on the whole I doubted it.

It wasn't long before we saw the range of mountains that form Mallorca's backbone gradually appearing in the distance. At first they looked as though they were distant shadows on the horizon and it was another half an hour before they took on substance. We could see the windmills on the central plain and cars chasing along the road into Palma. The boat moored neatly against the quay and the next stage in Adelfa's young life had begun.

28.
Aerial Exercises

Lisa drove the trailer off the ship without any mishaps, and Katherine and I climbed into our car to follow her to the farm. The road to Pollensa was slow and a bit tedious but that was fine because I was so relieved just to have completed the journey and to know that little Adelfa was in safe and secure hands. I'd always cared for her, but I'd become aware of three things.

The first was that love horses as I might, they always need specialist care and knowledge that I didn't possess. Secondly, I believed that Adelfa had the makings of a champion horse who could produce wonderful sons and daughters and thirdly, I was just plain glad I didn't have to walk that 15 kilometres again.

There was a fourth thing that nagged at the back of my brain. I was becoming aware that perhaps Ibiza, or my own circumstances, weren't right for what I had originally dreamed of – the breeding of Arab horses. I wasn't sure what was going to happen when we arrived in Pollensa but I was looking forward to it.

Mallorca was very different from Ibiza. There was a major city, Palma de Mallorca, with its own opera house, department stores, and a large harbour. Ibiza, on the other hand, had an old-fashioned cinema, numerous shops, *tiendas*, and a smallish port where the ferries dropped anchor and swung round to tie up alongside the jetty.

Mallorca had a chain of mountains culminating in the highest peak, Puig Mayor which scaled some 1,500 metres, whereas Ibiza had a single peak called Sa Atalaya which reached around only 470 metres and a whole host of rounded hillocks; Mallorca was home to a wine industry while Ibiza produced a very acceptable *hierbas* and some intensely undrinkable *vino pajes*, a country wine that you would have had to be desperate to want more of than just a small tumbler. As we drove northeast towards Pollensa, I was aware that while there were some similarities with the countryside of Ibiza, the flat plain in the centre of Mallorca was much bigger than the equivalent on the smaller island. The central region outside Palma was home to hundreds of windmills, some in reasonable condition, some completely decrepit.

I was looking forward to exploring our temporary home and to finding out more about the island. The culture of the two islands was intertwined and yet there were vast differences. I recalled having a drink in a bar and asking an Ibicenco from Santa Eulalia about the languages spoken in the two islands. I said that obviously, from the point of view of a foreigner, they were very similar and both offshoots of the Catalan spoken in the region around Barcelona. He'd stared at me as though I was out of my mind. "*Señor,*" he replied, "*Somos Ibicencos.* We are *Ibicencos.* Ibiza and Formentera, our sister island, form the Pitiuses Islands. We are not part of anything else and our language is our own."

I apologised profusely and pointed out that at the time, I was a newcomer to the island and didn't understand. Of course, with the typical courtesy of the Ibicenco, he smiled and invited me to a drink. Talking of courtesy, some years later, I was driving through Ibiza town when an Ibicenco in another car cut across the front of mine. I hooted and lent out of the window to shout at him. Actually, I translated as best I could a particularly nasty phrase from English to Spanish and this caused him to brake just ahead of me and to block the road in the process. He climbed out, shut his door and strode over. Bending down, he asked, "What was that you just said?"

Somewhat embarrassed, I repeated it. He looked shocked and said, "Where are you from? You're not Spanish." I admitted I was English.

"That was a terrible thing," he said. "We would never say such a thing here. Oh well, since otherwise you speak not bad Spanish and there's plenty of room to park both the cars, why don't we just go and have a beer and forget about it?" Of such incidents were friendships made in Ibiza. You were easily forgiven for human frailties and I just hoped it would be the same on Mallorca.

Arriving at Lisa's farm, we led Adelfa from the trailer and into a clean and spacious stable. She was capable, at times, of being the most irascible of animals and at others, and for no particular reason, sweet natured and gentle. On this occasion, she ambled quietly into the stable, inspected her new surroundings, gave a deep-throated rumble of approval and decided to have a light snack of some alfalfa. Clearly the new conditions suited her. We all leant on the stable door and admired her. "She's really a beautiful horse," commented Lisa. "Such enormous eyes, they're really amazing." We shut her in and tiptoed quietly away for a drink to celebrate our arrival.

I'd rented a small *finca* halfway between Pollensa town and Puerto Pollensa. It sat in a field just below the hills that ran up that side of the island. Scattered around were large and far smarter houses, most of them modern and owned by foreign residents. We knew a couple of them already from previous visits, in particular Geoff and Amanda who had retired to Mallorca after he'd made a fortune in the property business.

Our *finca* consisted of two bedrooms, a living room/kitchen and a bathroom with a shower. It seemed as though the house was simply some barns that had been 'improved' but it had electricity and running water as well as a chimney. Given that we weren't sure how long we'd stay in Mallorca, it seemed perfectly adequate. Besides, the weather was fine and dry and we didn't think that we'd be spending much time in the house.

Outside we had the use of the field that surrounded us and just above it we discovered a *torrente* that ran above and around the house. This was a deep gully that in summer was bone dry but in winter would channel away the water that ran off down the slope of the hills. It was filled with a large pile of rocks where a dry stone wall had collapsed and I made a mental note to talk to Francisco, our landlord, about clearing them away. It looked to me as if they could easily dam up the *torrente* causing it to overflow. If we had a bad enough autumn storm, the house could be in danger.

We unpacked, and then drove into Puerto Pollensa where we found a bar/restaurant that served the most delicious *sepia* (cuttlefish) in its own ink that I'd ever had. This was quite delicious and combined with a small green salad, a basket of fresh crusty bread and a bottle of strong red wine, it seemed like a good omen for our trip and we felt we were set up for an afternoon's exploration. We were due at Lisa's farm at about six but that left us enough time to drive back to Pollensa where we did some food shopping. It was there that we ran into Amanda and Geoff again.

Geoff was one of those people who was always going to be a success in life. The fact was that he started, developed and then sold his property business all in an amazingly short time and then decided he had absolutely no ambition whatsoever to rejoin the world's workers. Instead Amanda and he moved from their house in Hampshire to a flat in Florida and their house in Mallorca about once every three months with remarkably little fuss. They were intrigued with our story of Adelfa, longed for the day when she arrived in Pollensa and extended an open invitation to drop by at any time.

We ran into Geoff in the middle of the Plaza in front of the Church in the town about a week after we arrived. "Hello," he said, with his usual big beaming smile, "this is great, so you've arrived? That's wonderful, super, marvellous, marvellous, *so* glad to see you. Let's have a drink to celebrate shall we? Great, great, really glad." I suppose it was a completely unconscious habit but every time we met him, Geoff spent his time emphasising how absolutely superb and wonderful it all was. About ten minutes later Amanda appeared from a *tienda* and joined us. "Hello, darlings, this is all very pleasant. Are you free for supper this evening?"

"Yes," he chimed in, "do come, it would be marvellous, marvellous. We could have a swim first and then eat on the terrace. What fun, enormous, really great fun. We're so pleased to see you. Come about 5.30pm for drinks. Do say yes."

There wasn't much else we could possibly say but yes. It wasn't a hardship because they were really kind people and it was good to have them as near neighbours. We went a bit earlier to Lisa's to make sure all was well and then drove along the back *caminos* to Geoff and Amanda's enormous house. When we arrived, he was out on the terrace with a spider's web of cables laid out and what looked like a TV aerial in a million pieces spread all over the place.

"Hello," he said enthusiastically, "lovely to see you, so glad you could come, great."

Katherine asked him if he was putting up a TV aerial. "Yes, yes," he replied. "Bit of a dab hand at this sort of thing. Maybe you'd like to help?" he asked me.

"Yes, of course, anything I can do. I put our aerial up in Ibiza so this shouldn't be too difficult."

In no time at all we had the aerial connected to the co-axial cable and the main part of the contraption put together. Geoff had pre-drilled a hole through to the interior of the house so it was a simple matter of threading the cable through to the living room and attaching a co-axial cable connector to the end ready for connection to the television. Then it was a simple matter of using a couple of clamps to attach it to the pole.

"When's the chap coming to fix the aerial to the chimney? Shame to have everything ready except for that," I remarked innocently.

"Ah well," replied Geoff, peering intently at the toes of his *espadrilles*, "I thought perhaps you and I could do that part of it as well. It won't take 15 minutes, I've got the ladder and it will be great to get it done, really great, marvellous. You can always come up here and watch it too," he said, his voice trailing off slightly.

I'd never had problems with heights in any shape or form but I looked up at the pitched roof and realised it was some 40 feet up and not as comfortingly flat as our house in Ibiza. Still, it would seem churlish to refuse – so I agreed. We leant the ladder against the wall and Geoff suggested I should go up first, taking a rope attached to the aerial with me. He then explained that if I hauled the aerial up, he'd join me on the roof. The whole thing sounded highly dubious to me but up I went, rope in hand. I reached the top of the ladder that in turn just reached the edge of the roof. I managed to scramble up onto the 18-inch wide ledge that ran all the way round the house and cautiously straightened up. Behind me the tiles climbed away at the steep angle with a couple of chimneystacks sticking out.

"Marvellous, great, but be careful you don't tread on the *tejadas*, the terracotta tiles, they're old. Break one and we'll have real problems replacing it," bellowed Geoff. "Haul away, you'll soon have the aerial up there. I'll bring the tools and the fixings up with me."

Bit by bit the aerial came up to join me and I was finally able to place it gently on the roof behind me. "Here I come," shouted my fellow worker, "Move over a bit to your left so I can climb onto the ledge, there's masses of room, good, good, excellent." With that he arrived beside me wearing a strange-looking belt from which he'd hung a variety of tools. A large roll of heavy-duty galvanised wire hung from his left arm and from somewhere he'd acquired a hard hat. "Great," he enthused, "Look at that view, marvellous, you can see the sea from up here, fabulous. Right," he went on in his best Field Marshal's parade-ground voice, "Off we go, you lead on."

"Where?" I bleated, sounding more like a nervous sheep with every passing minute.

"Walk around the edge to that chimney stack. Come along, don't forget the aerial, I can't carry everything," he commanded, a note of irritation creeping into his voice.

I looked round at him in disbelief. The route along the ledge looked a mile long with the minute chimneystack poking up in the distance. It also involved turning through a right angle, or rather a left angle, to reach journey's end. "Are you sure this is such a good idea?" I quavered.

"Of course it is, it's marvellous, really excellent fun. No point in waiting for a local chap who'll charge the earth and won't turn up for six months," boomed Geoff. I could see why he'd made such a success of his business. No one would have dared do anything but obey. I heaved the aerial on its eight-foot pole upright and clutching it in front of me, I set off like a tightrope walker in a circus. The fact that the aerial threatened to tip me over the edge was neither here nor there, according to my Leader, marching close on my heels. "Come on, come on," he ordered impatiently, "we want to get down from here to have our swim before midnight." By this time, the only thing I wanted to do was to feel my feet safely on the ground and a large glass of something alcoholic in my hand.

Going round the corner was tricky to say the least as I swayed back and forth but eventually I lurched to a halt, put the wretched thing down carefully on the tiles and clung on to the chimneystack for dear life like a shipwrecked sailor clutching a life raft in the middle of a storm. Vertigo suddenly became a distinct possibility and I could well understand how it suddenly struck people who'd never suffered from it before. I peered into the far distance in the hope that I could kid myself it wasn't as bad as I feared, but one look down and I found myself swaying round and round.

"No time for doing your exercises," barked Geoff, "let's get on with it. You hold the pole against the chimneystack and I'll take care of attaching it. It'll soon be done."

Once again I heaved the pole upright and placed it against the brickwork. This meant that I could no longer hold on to anything else, and by now a breeze was starting to get up, making the aerial shudder like a yacht's mast in a gale.

"Can you get some of the wire round this before both the aerial and I take off and float away like Mary Poppins?" I asked him somewhat urgently.

"I'm going as fast as I can," Geoff replied, "but I think the cutters are still down on the terrace. I can't seem to find them anywhere." Dreadful thoughts chased through my mind as he scrabbled in his pockets. "Ah no, good, good, here they are in my shirt pocket. Now then, if we wind the wire around like this – can you hold it steady for a moment – and I twist the ends together, that's excellent. You can let go now." I took my hands away and the heavy pole and the aerial promptly shot sideways, giving Geoff a severe glancing blow over the head. Fortunately he was wearing the hard hat but now he lurched backwards towards the edge and it was by the merest chance that my outstretched hands grabbed his arm and managed to pull him back from the brink to the chimney, the hat wedged firmly down over his eyes. For a brief moment, we seesawed backwards and forwards until he was able to stand upright and pull the hat back up. "Geoff," I said through gritted teeth, "do you think we could get this blasted thing wired on properly as soon as possible and go back down? I really don't like it up here."

"Perhaps you're right, perhaps you're right," he muttered vaguely as I held the pole upright and he lashed it round with metre after metre of wire. The whole thing looked like a vast and demented spider had been weaving its web around the chimney but it seemed secure enough and I guessed you wouldn't be able to see it from the terrace. Finally the job seemed to be done and we then faced the problem of getting back to the ladder. Given that Geoff was still slightly groggy from the bash on the head, I insisted that once he'd packed all the tools back into his belt that he went first. We went crabwise towards the ladder, leaning on the sloping tile as we went. Finally we arrived, and I just about managed to hold the ladder so that he could climb down and he then did the same for me.

There was an indescribable sense of relief at being back on the terrace. I looked up at where we had been and thought it was a miracle that we'd both made it back down in one piece. Geoff still had a tendency to wander round in circles but apart from that he seemed all right. I went off in search of Amanda and Katherine and found them sitting by the pool, drinks in hand, discussing the colour of nail varnish.

"Hello," said Katherine, "you've been a long time for what must have been a pretty simple job? I mean, all you had to do was to fix the aerial up on the roof. Whatever took you so long?"

It's very hard to contain your feelings at such a moment without venting some colourful words, but I just about managed it. "You might want to go and make sure Geoff's OK," I said to Amanda. "He's had a smack over the head which nearly knocked him off the roof. Had it done so, he'd have landed somewhere near those oleanders." I pointed at some plants growing near the pool. Amanda gasped, leaped up and ran off in search of Geoff while I sat down, picked up Katherine's drink and downed it in one.

"Are you alright?" she asked looking at me doubtfully.

"No, not really. I think I've now got vertigo for the rest of my life, I've been chivvied along a narrow ledge carrying a ruddy great pole with a ruddy great aerial attached it and I don't ever want to do anything so silly again in what's left of my life. At this rate, I've used up about eight of my nine lives."

"So you're quite clear about that?" giggled Katherine. "I thought only cats had nine lives? I know you are quite capable of doing some dumb things but you should have seen yourself when you came round that corner. You looked like a dejected sparrow. Don't you think you ought to go in and clean yourself up before dinner?"

"Are we really staying for dinner?" I asked bitterly. "Knowing Geoff, he'll probably have us all doing a spot of fire walking across the barbecue as an aperitif before dinner. I'll stay on two conditions."

"What are they?" she asked

"That you promise never to allow Geoff to involve me in any harebrained schemes like that again and second that you get me a large glass full of red wine before I go inside."

As it turned out it was a memorable evening anyway. We had an excellent dinner and the only thing that dampened our host's spirits was the fact that despite having an aerial on the roof that would have helped make contact with Apollo 11 on its way to the moon, you could barely see anything of the programme through the vast amounts of interference on the screen. "It may be pointing in the wrong direction," commented Amanda.

"Good Lord, why on earth didn't we think of that before we came down? Tell you what, we've got a ruddy great torch. You wouldn't fancy popping up there with it and twiddling the pole while I sort out the picture down here? Geoff went on hopefully. "I feel that it needs my sort of skills to do that part of it down here and you were so good up there earlier. Like a blasted mountain goat, he was, skipping along the ledge. Didn't seem worried about the height at all." he said, turning to Amanda and Katharine.

"No," cried both the women rather in the manner of a Greek chorus.

"It's pitch black outside and he is *not* going up there again tonight, or indeed ever again," Katherine went on.

"Quite right," Amanda continued, "and neither are you, you half wit. We'll pay for a professional to come and do it. Widowhood wouldn't suit me just yet, thank you very much. I'm not saying it won't at some point but not tonight."

After a final cognac, we left for home at about 11.30pm with Geoff saying as we climbed in the car, "Lovely to see you, lovely, splendid. And thanks for helping out. Pity it doesn't work."

❧

We were driving along the road towards Puerto Pollensa when Katherine yelled at me to stop. I braked as fast as I could and leaping out of the car, she ran round to the front. I climbed out to see what was going on and found her crooning over a baby hedgehog cowering down in the car's headlights. His mother had decided to cross the road directly in front of the car and then abandoned her baby when she took fright. She'd legged it, as much as a hedgehog *can* leg it, into the grasses growing on the side of the road and there was no sign of her coming back.

"We can't just leave him," she said, "we'll have to take him home. I wonder what baby hedgehogs eat?"

"I know what they have and that's fleas," I replied. "Hang on, there a cardboard box in the boot. I'll get that."

And so we arrived home plus one baby hedgehog who was promptly christened Aerial. Katherine suggested Splendid or Marvellous but they seemed a bit too large for him. We thought of Geoff but he just didn't look like one. Aerial seemed to fit him best. We made a pen in the garden for him the following morning and he bumbled round it looking for all the world like an absent-minded professor who'd lost his glasses. We thinned out some milk and added some mince from the fridge on to a shallow plate. I vaguely remembered that hedgehogs also eat oats, so I took a small amount of fine oatmeal and mixed that in as well. Putting the dish down in his pen, we stepped back and waited to see what happened.

It looked as though it was more by accident than design that our new resident discovered his food. Clearly his mother had failed to teach him any table manners because having bumped into the edge and whiffled his nose in the direction of the mixture, he managed to lever his front end onto the edge and then, leg after leg, he heaved himself up onto the dish. Marching purposefully forward, Aerial waded into the middle of his breakfast, lowered his head and started to eat. By the time he decided he'd had enough, his belly and some of his little, pink rubbery spines were coated in the mixture. As he showed every sign of staying where he was, I picked him and put him into a small box we'd placed at the end of his run.

For some weeks our little friend lived what seemed to be a pretty good life. He liked nothing more than to lie on his back in the palm of your hand and have his tummy stroked. He'd close his eyes in ecstasy and his breathing would slow as he seemed to nod off. Obviously when he was abandoned by his mother, he hadn't yet learned to curl up when anything disturbed him.

Slowly his spines started to harden and he began to fill out and to grow towards adulthood. But there was a change in the weather, the evenings turned really cold and Aerial seemed pretty lethargic. It was as though he knew instinctively about hibernation and as it seemed too cold for him to stay outside, we filled a box with straw and took him into the shed next to our *finca*. It seemed to be the right sort of temperature and he certainly looked pretty comfortable. Every so often we'd lift him up gently just to make sure he was all right and we could just detect that he was breathing.

I checked with a nearby farmer to see if there was anything more we could have done and after looking at me as though I was slightly odd for wanting to save a baby hedgehog, he agreed that

Aerial's diet seemed to have been perfect and that he was well and truly sheltered for the duration of his first long snooze.

Sad to say, he never came out of hibernation. We noticed after a few weeks that there was a distinctly unpleasant smell when you went into the shed. I lifted Aerial out of the box and the smell grew worse. Clearly he was no longer in the land of the living but what on earth could have happened? I went back to the same farmer to see if he could shed any light on it. "*Bueno*," he said, "*la verdad es yo no se mucho de los erizos.* I don't know much about hedgehogs – I've never kept one – but I should think that there was something wrong with *el pequeño*, the little one, from the beginning and that is why his mother ran off."

I relayed this information to Katherine who looked very down in the mouth. "We must give him a proper burial," she insisted, and so we put him in the cardboard box filled with fresh straw, taped it up and then we went and dug a hole out in the field. In went Aerial and I covered him over with plenty of earth and then we went back to the house and drank a large toast to such a small and courageous animal.

29.

The Great Flood

The days were filled between exercising Adelfa and really getting to know the island. Our intention originally had been to spend perhaps a month on Mallorca while we saw how Adelfa settled in and then to make a decision about returning to Ibiza.

Lisa was proving to be a wonderful godmother to our little horse and I was becoming aware that for Adelfa to fulfil her potential, she would need to live in a set-up like SZED. I simply didn't have the wherewithal to achieve that in Ibiza and anyway, there weren't the stallions or the veterinary facilities available. And so we made the decision to stay on Mallorca for another two months to see how things went and then to decide whether we should return home or make the move permanent. This was obviously a major decision and not one that could be undertaken lightly.

Also I was starting to write regularly for a company that published guidebooks about destinations around the world and the one I was involved with was about Ibiza. This was another reason for needing to be in Ibiza, although a certain amount could be done based on my own knowledge. So all in all, the future was uncertain and the idea of not being with Adelfa after so much effort had gone into bringing her back to the Balearics was sad.

In the meantime, the colder weather was setting in and I'd been told that Mallorca in the wintertime could prove a lot chillier than Ibiza. The *finca* had a corner fireplace that looked slightly dubious given the amount of smoke that had stained the chimney breast, but to stay in the house we'd have to be able to use the fire so I spent a morning walking around the edge of the field. This provided me with quite a lot of usable firewood and I decided to give it a go. I did think of asking Geoff if he could give me a hand but then I realised he'd probably want to rebuild the entire fireplace and I'd end up on the roof putting up a new chimneystack.

There was no such thing as a grate, but it wasn't too difficult to figure out that by placing three rows of bricks in the hearth and then laying branches across them, air would be drawn from underneath and hopefully cause the fire to burn properly. I laid the fire and lit the layer of paper that in turn started the kindling burning.

The next part of the sequence was a fall of soot that covered the hearth, my feet and my trouser legs. It also effectively put out the fire. There are very few substances that smell, cling and stain as much as soot and this was no exception. However, by taking a torch and peering up the chimney, it was possible to see that it was now relatively clear, so having cleaned up the mess. I went through the whole procedure again.

After a couple of half-hearted flickerings and a curl of smoke that trickled lazily out of the hearth while the paper tried to decide whether it wanted to burn or not, the kindling caught and the room was made infinitely more cheerful. With the careful addition of a couple of thickish branches that I'd found under an almond tree, the house soon warmed up. "Wonderful," I thought, "that's one problem solved." I went over and closed the window that I'd opened to let out the smell of soot. This promptly caused a Vesuvius-like eruption of smoke from the fire that until now had been blazing away happily. It suddenly died down and looked sullen. Window open and it became cheerful and everything you could possibly ask of a fire. Window closed and like magic it decided that it had had enough thank you very much and would quite like to go out.

My heart sank and once again I left the window open. Now it was very much a question of whether the heat inside the room could overcome the cold air coming in. It also meant, judging by the speed the wood I'd put in at the start was being converted to ash that I was going to have to spend much of my time either cutting up tree trunks or going to a wood yard and buying logs. I opted for the latter as it was less time-consuming and after a quick trip to Lisa to find out where to head, I was on my way. The procedure was very much the same as back home in Ibiza except that the yard was larger and there was more pre-cut wood. As I loaded up, I made absolutely sure that there were no mice lurking nearby, waiting to cause me to have untold grey hairs.

It was just a matter of minutes and I was back in the car but this time I headed down to Inca and then on to the wine centre of the island, Binissalem. I'd been told that vine cultivation in Mallorca dated back certainly to around 100 BC and that not a great deal later, Pliny had written about the quality of wine from the Balearics. Sadly, according to my informant, at the end of the 19th century, the dreaded phylloxera had destroyed much of the island's vines and it wasn't until two-thirds of the way through the 20th century, thanks to a great deal of effort on the part of the wine producers that things really picked up, to the point where, around 15 years ago, the Binissalem region was awarded the *Denominacio D'Origen* or Denomination of Origin (DO). I wanted to buy some supplies for the *finca* and I was also looking for a really inexpensive red that I could use for making mulled wine. There was a chill in the air and it was time to get a pan on the stove and start a brew. Besides, Geoff and Amanda had said they might drop in and I wanted to be prepared.

My rooftop companion advised knocking a hole through the living room wall to provide a draught and after an evening of discussion they left around midnight. Big fat drops of rain had been spattering down all evening and there were the occasional flashes of lightning and rumbles of thunder. It was good to have the fire burning and the house cosy. Because the field sloped quite steeply, there were steps down from each room till you came to the living room at the bottom and this meant the heat warmed each room as it rose up to the top.

At about three in the morning, I was awakened by a very strange rushing sound. In exactly the same way that it would have done in Ibiza, the power had gone off leaving the house in pitch darkness and I reached for the torch we kept by the bed. I couldn't find it so I threw back the covers and stepped out of bed. The shock was quite literally staggering. I had put my feet down into around half a metre of freezing cold water that seemed to be pouring down through the house. It was so cold I couldn't even swear. This wasn't any simple leak from the roof, this was quite serious and I figured I'd better find out where it was coming from in double quick time.

I woke Katherine up, unintentionally, by dripping water on her as I shook her awake. "Whaaa?" she asked in that way that most of us do when we are woken up in the middle of the night.

"We've got a problem. There seems to be water in the house," I replied in my best 'Every man must do his duty' voice.

"Well of course there is. We've got a bathroom. You must have left a tap on. Go and turn it off." And with that she started to drift off to sleep again.

"No, no!" I yelped, "don't doze off again. There's water flooding through from top to bottom. At this rate, we could drown."

Katherine sat bolt upright and said, "Whatever are you talking about? And why don't you put the light on? And what's that noise that sounds like running water?"

"Listen to me. The power's off and there's water coming in from the top and by the sound of it, gushing down to the living room. I'm going to try and find out where it's coming from"

"Well, for heaven's sake, put something on," she said sleepily. "It's freezing cold."

Irrationally, I put on a T-shirt and a pair of boots. Given that my footwear came up to just above my ankle and the water reached up to just below my knee, it was pretty reasonable to assume that my feet were going to continue to get wet.

"Stay there till I find out what it is," I suggested, as I sloshed my way out of the bedroom and up the stairs to the back door. This was where I made a considerable mistake. I should have opened the door at the bottom of the house, working on the theory that gravity would take the water out from the bottom level. Instead, as I pulled aside the top door, the flood redoubled its efforts and by now it was reaching rather higher than my kneecaps.

Fortunately the torch had two things in its favour. The first was that it was clad in rubber and so it was waterproof; the second was that it was shockproof so that when I dropped it in surprise at the sudden influx of muddy, horrible, pebble laden water, it didn't go out and I was able to see where it was. From the bedroom floated a hopeful female voice asking, "What are you doing?"

Using a fair amount of strength I managed to push the door shut, after clearing a pile of small stones that had become wedged in the doorway, picked up the torch and waded back to the bedroom. The stairs had become distinctly slippery but I reached the door and peered in at Katherine who seemed to have gone back to sleep. In another five minutes I figured the water would reach the bottom of the bed and so I trudged down to the bottom door and tugged and bashed it open. It was bit like those films where they open the sluice gates in a dam and a spout of water gushes out. Suddenly the level in the living room dropped by a good 20 centimetres and although it continued to flow through the house, there was less to contend with. The problem was that on the inner side of the living room door was a step some 15 centimetres in depth so I realised there'd definitely be water left behind in the room that had to be bailed out.

Nevertheless, whatever I did, it was clear that I had to try and divert the flow at the top so I went outside to take a look. I hadn't noticed the gap under the upper door before and it was obvious what needed to be done. I remember seeing an old sheet of tin in the shed and it was the work of a minute to collect a hammer and the tin sheet and to wedge it against the door. The next thing I needed was a couple of hefty stones to hold it in place and there were plenty of these on the edge of the *torrente.*

Still wearing just a T-shirt and the boots, I staggered up to the bridge and it was there that I realised what had happened. The half-witted landlord had left the *torrente* filled with boulders and, just as I'd predicted, the first storm of the winter had arrived filling the channel until it became a foaming torrent. Given that the ground was bone dry, the water had taken the line of least resistance, breached the bank and poured down to the house. By now, water was arriving from a fair few hillsides in the Pollensa area and taking a minor diversion through our rented house on its way to the sea.

Gathering up as many large stones as I could manage, I trudged back to the door and hammered the rocks in place causing the water to make an irritable gurgle as it was diverted away from the interior of the house. Making my way back down to the lower door, I splashed my way inside to find that the flow of water had slowed to a trickle coming from the other rooms. There was a bucket and a dustpan in the kitchen and having collected these, I went back and started bailing out the living room, feeling like the Ancient Mariner.

After about 15 minutes, there was about an inch of water left in the room when Katherine came out of the bedroom rubbing her eyes.

"Whatever are you doing banging about and washing the floor in the middle of the night by torchlight and wearing such strange clothing? You'll have ruined those boots, sloshing water all over them."

I'd was familiar with the expression 'words failed me' but this was the first time it had happened to me. I was frozen to the marrow, soaking wet and I'd spent three quarters of an hour following the example of King Canute when he tried to stem the tide and yet Katherine thought I'd been washing the floor while she slept the sleep of the just.

"Oh well," she went on, "I'll make us a cup of tea, now we're both awake."

☙

By 7am there was some semblance of order in the house, the last of the water had gone and somehow I'd managed to coax a somewhat sullen fire into life that was beginning to dry things out. I was drinking my third cup of tea and mulling over what dreadful thing I could do to our landlord when there was tentative tap on the door. I still hadn't put on any other clothing, so I peered round the door. Outside stood a Mallorquin that I hadn't met before. "*Buenos dias, Señor*," he said, turning his beret in his hands. "I have been sent to see you by the *Señor* who lives in the big white house on the hill behind you." He pointed towards a largish house about half a kilometre away and much further up than us.

"He is a foreign *Señor*, and he wondered if you would like to come to breakfast. He heard the storm and thought you might need some help. If there is anything I can do here, please tell me."

"You're very kind but I think we can manage. We've cleaned up the worst of the damage. We had water flowing through the house that damaged quite a lot of our things but I managed to stop it in the end by putting a sheet of metal across the top door." A thought suddenly struck me. "Could you wait a minute while I put on some clothes?" I quickly went into the bedroom, threw on some old jeans and went back to our visitor. Going outside, I shook his hand and introduced myself. We started to walk up towards the bridge as I asked, "Do you know if this has happened before? In the middle of the night I saw the water coming from the *torrente* in this direction and I think it was the fact that there were large stones blocking the *torrente* that caused the water to come in this direction."

The stranger stopped and turned to me, looking embarrassed. "I shouldn't say it but the owner of the *finca* where you are staying, he is not a good man and he does not care. The water has come into the house many times and each time he cleans it up and then he rents it out to somebody else. Yes, it is the *piedras*, the stones that cause the problem and he is too lazy to remove them."

"Thank you for telling me," I replied. "I'm very grateful to know that and when I meet the owner I shall know how to deal with him. And the *Señor* who lives up on the hill, is he English?"

"*Ay, no no, Señor*. He is very old and he is *un caballero*, a gentleman from Russia. He has lived here many years and *mi esposa*, my wife who cleans the house for him, tells me he was a relative of *El Rey*, the King of Russia, how do you say, the Czar? But now he is very poor and not in good health. The house is big and he cannot afford to heat it properly. But he would be very happy if you would go and see him – and maybe you and the *Señora* could warm yourselves a little?"

"We'd be very grateful. I don't know your name."

"My apologies, *Señor* my name is Ramón."

"And I am Stewart. *Es un nombre escoces*, a Scottish name. Some people call me Eduardo and mi *Señora* is called Katerina. Would you be kind enough to say that we'll be there about 8am and would you say to the *Señor* that we are very sorry for the way we look? We still don't have any electricity so we can't heat any water."

Ramón looked upset once again. "*Esta ridiculo, este tio...* I am sorry, I'm annoyed with the owner of the *finca*. There is a box that contains *fusibles*, fuses, in the shed outside. Did he not show you? Of course not. He is a bad man. Come, we will see if a *fusible* is broken."

We went down into the shed and he pulled aside boxes that were blocking a small, wall-mounted cupboard. Inside, there was an ancient fuse box filled with the most dreadful looking porcelain monstrosities that appeared old enough to have come out of Noah's Ark. Ramón tugged and wrestled each one out of its socket until finally, with a grunt, he came to one where the wire was broken. "*Mira, Señor*, look, this is the one that is causing the problem with your electricity. Now we have to see whether this *hijo de puta*, this son of a whore, has had the sense to keep some spare wire. He scrabbled around until he came to a small piece of card with thin wire wrapped around it.

He pulled a worn pocket knife out of his trouser pocket, cut off a length of fuse wire, used the small screwdriver on the side of the knife to undo the connections on the fuse and pulled out the broken ends. It was the work of a moment to put the new wire in place, tighten the screws and push the fuse back into the socket in the box.

There was a yelp of surprise from inside the house as Katherine discovered that the power had come on. "I'm very grateful, Ramón, I wouldn't have known where to look at all. I can't thank you enough."

"*Es nada,* I will go now and tell the *Señor* that you will come up at about 8am" We waved at each other as he crossed the bridge over the *torrente* and I went inside to tell Katherine to prepare herself for breakfast with a member of the Russian Royal Family.

30.
Going Home

W e were a fashionable ten minutes late as we parked the car and climbed the steps to an imposing oak front door. I banged on the knocker and seconds later it was opened by Ramón. "*Bienvenido, Señores*, welcome. *Señor* Daniel is waiting for you in the *sala*. Please, follow me."

He led us along a wide, gloomy hallway that was lined with portraits and framed documents and turned into an equally dark room. A small fire was burning in an enormous chimney and an elderly man was sitting with a rug over his knees.

"Good morning," he smiled. "Do please come in. Forgive me for not getting up. My knees are very stiff these days but Ramón will help you to pull up chairs so that we can enjoy the heat of the fire." His English was impeccable but it was overlaid with an incredibly heavy accent.

We settled ourselves near to him and he went on, "My name is Daniel, as I believe Ramón mentioned. And your wife's name?"

"This is Katherine and my name is Stewart," I replied.

"Oh, I understood your name to be Eduardo," he said in surprise in a rich, dark brown sort of voice that sounded thick with those cigarettes that are packed with heavy smelling Russian tobacco that's been washed down with regular shots of vodka.

I explained that sometimes Spaniards couldn't manage my name and I'd become accustomed to being called Eduardo. "I shall call you Stewart," he laughed. "I knew a number of people called Stewart when I was a translator in Washington. That was a long time ago, of course. I have lived in Mallorca for many years now, and I have to say that you are not the first people to have suffered flooding in that little *finca*. When the rain started so heavily last night, I thought there might be problems for you and then I saw your flashlight when I looked out of my bedroom window in the middle of the night. I trust that the flooding has not incommoded you too much?"

"We've lost a certain amount of clothes," I explained, "as well as some family photographs which is much worse. It's incredible that the owner of the property doesn't resolve the problem once and for all. I can't wait to get hold of him."

At this moment, Ramón came in carrying a tray with a coffee pot, cups, sugar and hot milk and a plate of *ensaimadas,* the pastry we were used to in Ibiza. He spent a little time distributing the contents of the tray so I bent down and produced from my *cesta,* my basket, a bottle of cognac. "Would you think me very rude if we all had some with our coffees?" I asked our host tentatively.

He laughed delightedly. "I would not think you rude. I would only be insulted if you didn't offer me some. Also, it might help to warm us all up. You are very Spanish, my friend! You have lost your, how should I say, your Englishness."

I suggested to Daniel that Ramón might care for some as well. "You were so kind to repair our electricity," I went on. "We'd never have found it without you."

"Yes Ramón, get another cup and we shall celebrate you as the bringer of light."

And so we spent a very pleasant hour with Daniel. Eventually, Ramón slipped out and just before we left, I took the plunge and said, "I understand from Ramón that you were born in Russia. May I ask when you left?"

"Ah, another part of my life,", the old man murmured, staring intently into the flames. His voice saddened as he explained, "It was 1918 before I was able to escape via the Crimea. I made my way to Istanbul and eventually to America. As I mentioned before, I was a translator for the State Department in the United States for many years but my wife and I always yearned to return to Europe to live. I would have been happy to have returned to

Russia but it was never possible with my family connections. You will see why if you look at some documents when you go out into the hall."

"And your wife?" asked Katherine softly.

"Ah, she died a few years ago. I still miss her very much. She was wonderful and we were very much in love always. Also, I don't have a great deal of money these days and so life has become a little difficult. Ramón and his wife are very kind to me. Without them, I don't know what I would do."

As we took our leave, we thanked him for his hospitality and promised to return in the next few days. I managed to leave the bottle of brandy down by the chair leg. Ramón was waiting by the front door and I asked him to ensure that Daniel drank some of it. "He told us he doesn't have much money? Does he have enough to heat the house?"

"*Señor*, he eats very little and there is not much money for heating. He sits by the chimney almost all day to keep warm. My *Señora* and I try to do what we can. We have a piece of land in the country and we bring back what firewood that we can find. He will be very glad of the cognac. I will make sure he has some in his coffee."

❧

We drove off down the hill in the direction of our house. There was a silence between us. Meeting Daniel and seeing his circumstances had saddened us both and combined with the worry of the flood, we didn't feel in the mood for laughter. I dropped Katharine at the house and went off to Lisa's farm to check on Adelfa. I parked the car and went over to the corral where the little mare was gazing thoughtfully at the hills in the distance. I just stood and watched her for a few minutes and she became aware of my presence.

Slowly the little horse turned and ambled up to the fence. She blew out through her nostrils at me and peered hopefully at my jacket in case I had any treats hidden there. I slipped under the top rail and climbed into the ring as she came closer and rested her muzzle on my chest. This was a signal that she required a gentle scratch behind her ears. I took her head in my arms and asked her, "What should I do about you, little one? Would you be happier here? Is this where your future lies?" It might have been a coincidence but she shook her head up and down as though agreeing with me. I knew that Lisa would give her the best of homes and Adelfa could really achieve all the potential she had in her.

But then I wondered why I had gone through that crazy journey on the train, all the time in Ibiza and all those weird walks up and down the *camino* to the port. Perhaps sometimes it's best not to look too deeply into those things – but it still seemed strange. Something inside me said that the best thing I could do would be to leave her here, if Lisa agreed to it. I tickled under Adelfa's mane and then I ran off across the corral. She gallumphed after me in a cross between a trot and a canter, looking for all the world like a rocking horse. It was almost as though she was laughing at me as we reached the other side and I slipped through the rails again. I decided in that moment that I would find Lisa and see how she felt about adopting a small, grey Arab mare into her herd.

As it turned out, the same thoughts had been going through Lisa's head and the arrangement was made without any difficulty. "I promise," she said over a drink, "that she'll have the best possible attention and who knows, she might turn out to be a little star when she gets around to breeding. In the meantime, I've got the blacksmith coming tomorrow to change her shoes. Do you want to give me a hand?"

We arranged that I'd be on the farm by 10am and I went back to our house to tell Katharine about the conversation. "However sad it is, I really think it's for the best," she said. "Lisa's set-up is so perfect and it would be the best for Adelfa."

We spent the rest of the day finishing with the cleaning up and, as the decision was made about the mare, I went off to Palma to find out about tickets for us for the return journey to Ibiza. It turned out that there were places on the boat four days later and so, with a heavy heart, I bought the tickets. It seemed very strange to be returning without her and I couldn't imagine how I was going to tell Antonio about my decision but part of me knew that it was right.

The following morning, the sky was that stunningly clear blue that you get in the Balearics in the autumn. We stopped off in Pollensa for a *carajillo* and as we sat down at the bar, Geoff and Amanda came round the corner. "My dears," she cried, "we've heard about what happened to you. You were flooded out. How awful."

"Awful, awful," he echoed, "dreadful, dreadful, dreadful. Would you like me to come round and see if we can fix things up a bit? Maybe we could waterproof things a bit. Wouldn't that be splendid?"

Having thanked Geoff profusely for his kind offer, I went on to explain to them the conversation about Adelfa and the subsequent decision about returning to Ibiza. "Oh no, that's so sad. We've only just met and now you're leaving again. I can't bear it. I really can't bear it." Geoff looked so totally downcast that I pointed out, "It gives you the most perfect excuse to come and see us in Ibiza however."

"How splendid, marvellous, marvellous. I think this calls for a drink. Shall we set a date now? Excellent, never been to Ibiza."

"Calm down, darling, they haven't gone yet. We're all going to Lisa's to watch Adelfa being shod. Come along, Geoff, finish your drink. The blacksmith will be arriving at any moment," Amanda said, urging her husband up from his chair.

As it happened, the blacksmith dead-heated with us as we all arrived at the farm and we saw that Adelfa was standing calmly in an open stable. Juan unloaded the tools of his trade while Geoff and Angela went and cooed over the mare and I went off to the house to find Lisa to let her know that there was a rather larger shoeing party than she'd figured on. This didn't faze her in the least and we made our way back to the stable to greet Juan.

He set out his tools and we gathered round Adelfa. "*Que te parece*, what do you think, *Señor*, could you hold her hind leg up while I attach the shoe?"

"*Nigun problema,*" I replied moving to the mare's back end. I bent down in the posture that's guaranteed to put your back out, took the appropriate leg in my hands and lifted it carefully onto my knee. With an irritable shake of her leg, Adelfa swatted me off in much the same way that I would do if a mosquito landed on my arm.

"No, no *Señor*, you must hold the leg of *la yegua* firmly so that she cannot do that," grinned Juan. "Please pick it up again."

Having first picked myself up, I returned to my little horse, went through the same procedure and once again, I landed in roughly the same spot. "I wonder what you're doing that's wrong?" asked Geoff helpfully.

"I'm not convinced I'm doing anything wrong," I replied through gritted teeth as I clutched my aching back. "Perhaps you'd like a go?" I enquired.

"Ah, well, yes, yes, I'd love to actually. I'm sure it all comes down to the holding technique. Yours looked all wrong, absolutely wrong. Also, I'm exceptionally strong and not afraid of things like a horse's hind legs." We all stood and watched in amazement as he marched over the little mare's head, wagged his finger under her muzzle and addressed her forcefully. "Now then, young lady, I don't want any nonsense of that sort with me. I shan't stand for it, believe you me. Understood?"

Adelfa lowered her head and gave a moody tug at a wisp of hay that she'd found. To everyone's surprise Geoff, having located himself next to one of her hind legs, gave a sharp tug, the leg came up and rested on his knee and Juan was able to fit the appropriate shoe. He looked at me and smiled. "*¡Este Señor sabe mucho de los caballos!* This *Señor* know a lot about horses. Let's get the next one on quickly."

Looking distinctly pleased with himself, Geoff marched quickly round to the other leg, bent down and with the same firm lifting motion, he placed her limb on his knee. Once again, Juan worked swiftly and Geoff released the leg. It was at this moment that the problem came. When he tried to stand upright his back, as he told us later, had locked for the first time in his life. Lurching backwards bent over at a very odd right-angle, he let out a cry that sounded like a beginner trying to play an un-tuned violin. "Owwwwwww!" he screeched, "Oh, my back, my back, my back." The shock was so great that he reached behind to try and grasp the afflicted part and instead clutched onto the upper part of Adelfa's leg. Already unnerved by the eldritch scream, she clearly objected to a strange pair of hands grabbing at that part of her anatomy. She'd had enough … and with a smart backwards motion she managed to send Geoff headlong into a pile of hay.

Confusion reigned for a few moments as various voices were raised. "The blasted animal has killed me," came a muffled cry from our great hero as he tried to extract his head from the hay. "No she hasn't or you wouldn't be making such a racket," came from his somewhat unsympathetic wife. "Get up and stop playing the fool."

Juan, in his turn, cried out, "Mind the *yegua,* he mustn't be allowed to hurt the horse," while Lisa, Katherine and I looked at each other and bit our lips to stop uncontrollable laughter breaking out.

Eventually order was restored with Geoff being helped into the house where he swore that it had been an unprovoked attack on Adelfa's part and the only thing that would restore his health, his confidence in himself as a horseman and begin to heal his back was the first of a series of tumblers of neat brandy with a couple of painkillers. He was obviously going to make the most of it and the story of how he had been attacked by a giant ravening horse foaming at the mouth would definitely grow and multiply over the years. We all felt considerable sympathy for Amanda as it was becoming plain that in Geoff's mind, teams of surgeons might well be required to put him back on his feet. In the meantime, Juan and I had completed the job of shoeing *la yegua* and we led her out into the paddock. Slipping the rein from her head collar, we let her loose and off she careered bucking and kicking like a young foal.

Lunch was rather dominated by the drama of Geoff's back as he sat slumped forward over his plate. Occasionally he would let out piteous groans as he lifted remarkably large quantities of food into his mouth for a man who had supposedly been killed an hour or two earlier. The talk turned to our intention of returning to Ibiza. "We'd like to come and visit you," said our invalid, "but only on the condition that you haven't any other horses."

The remaining days slipped by and soon we were packing our car with the possessions that remained after the flood. We'd been in Mallorca for a total of around two months, we'd met some wonderful people and had a number of, to say the least, unusual experiences. The day before we left, I took the remains of our firewood and various bottles of whisky, brandy and gin up to Daniel's house. Ramón answered the door and showed me into the sitting room. It was as though Daniel hadn't moved in the days since we had first met him. "I'm very sorry that you are leaving," he said quietly. "I shall miss your visits and especially the very kind, er, gifts that you have managed to leave behind. It is a shame that one so young should have such a bad memory!"

"I've brought a few more things," I explained. "I wondered if it would be alright the next time we are in Mallorca if we came and saw you?"

"I would be most disappointed if you didn't," he responded, smiling at me. "So we can say this is only a temporary farewell then?"

I stood up to go and as he clasped my hand, he pulled me down to his height and gave me an embrace. "*Vaya con Dios,*" he murmured, "go with God." Ramón came down to the car and helped me to unload the firewood. "I would like to come down later on this morning to say goodbye to you and the *Señora,*" he said. "We'll miss you both."

Two more things of note happened before we left. I was standing outside the house trying to figure out how I could squeeze one last suitcase of clothes into the boot of the car when a car came hurtling down the *camino* and screeched to a halt. Out jumped our landlord, Francisco, clearly in a bad mood and trailing a hefty aroma of something alcoholic. "They say you are leaving," he shouted. "you are *ladrones*, you are thieves. You owe me one more month of money before you go. You rented the house for three months."

As I was about to answer him, Ramón emerged from the front door. He'd arrived about half an hour before and was having a last drink with us. "I heard what you just said to this *Señor,*" he said quietly, "and I think *you* should apologise."

"What should I apologise for?" shouted Francisco. "He owes me money and look, his car is full. Obviously they are leaving. Fortunate for me that I was able to get here in time to stop them."

"Once again, you have rented the house out to people who have had problems with the property. You know what happens when the *torrente* fills up, you know how the house floods and you've heard how much these *Señores* have lost. And all of this because you are too lazy and you drink too much to clear the *torrente*. Apologise now or you will have me to deal with. I will report you to the *Policia* and make a *denuncia* for your behaviour in demanding money in a threatening manner."

For a moment Francisco swayed slightly as he glared at me while he clearly debated whether it was worthwhile continuing with the row. He turned and stared angrily at Ramón, and then turning on his heel he stumped off to his car muttering to himself. "Thank you Ramón, that was very kind of you. I probably would have given him the money if you hadn't been here," I said.

Eventually Ramón took his leave and we went one last time to check on the *Correos*, to see if any post had arrived. I found we'd received a card from a friend who lived near us in Ibiza. The cover was a picture of the roof of the church in Santa Eulalia. Inside it said, *Felices Fiestas*, Season's Greetings. This struck me as odd given that it was only October, but as he explained to me later, it was the only one he had to hand. Also, time in Ibiza moves in mysterious ways. The message he'd written inside made the greatest of great good sense. Quite simply it said:

'East, West, Ibiza's Best'

We felt that the timing for the card was right and though we were leaving Adelfa behind, we knew that it was for the best.

Although I felt enormously sad at going, I was returning home to the island that was really a part of me. It was a time of change and I looked forward to getting on with the guidebook and seeing all the friends we'd left behind for the last two months.

❧

We drove one last time down the Pollensa to Palma road in plenty of time to catch the ferry. This departed on time and it was with a real sense of excitement that we saw Ibiza as it appeared through the mist. In no time the ship was tying up against the quay and down below us there were the usual people waving to relatives who had braved the outside world and others who would be boarding the ship for its return journey to Palma. I looked up at D'Alt Vila at the top of the hill and the small white houses of the La Marina district tumbling down the foot of the hill and it felt good to be home.

THE END

BUYING A HOME SERIES

Our 'Buying a Home' books, including *Buying, Selling & Letting Property*, are essential reading for anyone planning to purchase property abroad. They're packed with vital information to guide you through the property jungle and help you **avoid the sort of disasters that can turn your dream home into a nightmare!** Topics covered include:

- **Avoiding problems**
- **Choosing the region**
- **Finding the right home and location**
- **Estate agents**
- **Finance, mortgages and taxes**
- **Utilities, heating and air-conditioning**
- **Renting and letting**
- **Permits and visas**
- **Travelling and communications**
- **Health and insurance**
- **Renting a car and driving**
- **Retirement and starting a business**
- **And much, much more!**

Our 'Buying a Home' books are the most comprehensive and up-to-date source of information available about buying property abroad. Whether you want a detached house, a townhouse or an apartment, a holiday or a permanent home, these books will help make your dreams come true.

They will also save you time, trouble and money!

Order your copies today by phone, fax, post or email from: Survival Books, PO Box 3780, YEOVIL, BA21 5WX, United Kingdom (☎/▤ +44 (0)1935-700060, ✉ sales@survivalbooks.net, 🖥 www.survivalbooks.net).

LIVING AND WORKING SERIES

Our 'Living and Working' books are essential reading for anyone planning to spend time abroad, including holiday-home owners, retirees, long-term visitors, business people, transferees, students and even extra-terrestrials! They're packed with important and useful information designed to help you **avoid costly mistakes and save both time and money.** Topics covered include how to:

- **Find a job with a good salary & conditions**
- **Avoid and overcome problems**
- **Find your dream home**
- **Get the best education for your family**
- **Make the best use of public transport**
- **Endure local motoring habits**
- **Obtain the best health treatment**
- **Stretch your money further**
- **Make the most of your leisure time**
- **Enjoy the local sporting life**
- **Find the best shopping bargains**
- **Insure yourself against most eventualities**
- **Do numerous other things not listed above**

Our 'Living and Working' books are the most comprehensive and up-to-date source of practical information available about everyday life abroad. They aren't, however, boring text books, but interesting and entertaining guides written in a highly readable style. **Read these books and discover what it's *really* like to live and work abroad!**

Order your copies today by phone, fax, post or email from: Survival Books, PO Box 3780, YEOVIL, BA21 5WX, United Kingdom (☎/🖨 +44 (0)1935-700060, ✉ sales@survivalbooks.net, 🖥 www.survivalbooks.net).

OTHER SURVIVAL BOOKS

Alien's Guides: The Alien's Guides to Britain and France will help you to appreciate the peculiarities (in both senses) of the British and French.

The Best Places to Buy a Home in France/Spain: The most comprehensive and up-to-date guides to where to buy property in France and Spain, containing detailed regional profiles.

Buying, Selling and Letting Property: The most comprehensive and up-to-date source of information on buying, selling and letting property in the UK.

Earning Money From Your Home: Essential guides to earning income from property in France and Spain, including short- and long-term letting.

Foreigners in France/Spain: Triumphs & Disasters: Real-life experiences of people who have emigrated to France and Spain, recounted in their own words.

Lifeline Guides: Essential guides to life in specific regions of France and Spain. See order form for a list of current titles in the series.

Making a Living: Essential guides to self-employment and starting a business in France and Spain.

Renovating & Maintaining Your French Home: The ultimate guide to renovating and maintaining your dream home in France.

Retiring: Retiring in Spain and Retiring in France provide up-to-date information about the two most popular retirement destinations.

Rural Living in France: The most comprehensive source of practical information available about life in rural France.

Shooting Caterpillars in Spain: The hilarious but compelling story of two innocents abroad in the depths of Andalusia in the late '80s.

Surprised by France: Even after living there for ten years, Donald Carroll finds plenty of surprises in the Hexagon.

Order your copies today by phone, fax, post or email from: Survival Books, PO Box 3780, YEOVIL, BA21 5WX, United Kingdom (☎/▤ +44 (0)1935-700060, ✉ sales@survivalbooks.net, ▣ www.survivalbooks.net).

Qty	Title	Price (incl. p&p)			Total
		UK	Europe	World	
	The Alien's Guide to Britain	£7.45	£9.45	£12.95	
	The Alien's Guide to France	£7.45	£9.45	£12.95	
	The Best Places to Buy a Home in France	£14.45	£16.45	£19.95	
	The Best Places to Buy a Home in Spain	£14.45	£16.45	£19.95	
	Buying a Home in Australia & NZ	£14.45	£16.45	£19.95	
	Buying a Home in Bulgaria	£14.45	£16.45	£19.95	
	Buying a Home in Cyprus	£14.45	£16.45	£19.95	
	Buying a Home in Florida	£14.45	£16.45	£19.95	
	Buying a Home in France	£15.45	£17.45	£20.95	
	Buying a Home in Greece	£14.45	£16.45	£19.95	
	Buying a Home in Italy	£14.45	£16.45	£19.95	
	Buying a Home in Portugal	£14.45	£16.45	£19.95	
	Buying a Home in South Africa	£14.45	£16.45	£19.95	
	Buying a Home in Spain	£15.45	£17.45	£20.95	
	Buying, Selling & Letting Property	£12.45	£14.45	£17.95	
	Buying or Renting a Home in London	£14.45	£16.45	£19.95	
	Buying or Renting a Home in New York	£14.45	£16.45	£19.95	
	Earning Money From Your French Home	£14.45	£16.45	£19.95	
	Earning Money From Your Spanish Home	£14.45	£16.45	£19.95	
	Foreigners in France: Triumphs & Disasters	£12.45	£14.45	£17.95	
	Foreigners in Spain: Triumphs & Disasters	£12.45	£14.45	£17.95	
	Brittany Lifeline	£12.45	£14.45	£17.95	
	Costa Blanca Lifeline	£12.45	£14.45	£17.95	
	Costa del Sol Lifeline	£12.45	£14.45	£17.95	
	Dordogne/Lot Lifeline	£12.45	£14.45	£17.95	
	Normandy Lifeline	£12.45	£14.45	£17.95	
	Poitou-Charentes Lifeline	£12.45	£14.45	£17.95	
	Provence-Cote d'Azur Lifeline	£12.45	£14.45	£17.95	
	Living & Working in America	£17.45	£19.45	£22.95	
	Living & Working in Australia	£17.45	£19.45	£22.95	
	Living & Working in Britain	£17.45	£19.45	£22.95	
	Living & Working in Canada	£17.45	£19.45	£22.95	
	Living & Working in the EU	£17.45	£19.45	£22.95	
	Living & Working in the Far East	£17.45	£19.45	£22.95	
	Living & Working in France	£17.45	£19.45	£22.95	
	Living & Working in Germany	£17.45	£19.45	£22.95	
				Total	

ORDER FORM

Qty	Title	Price (incl. p&p)			Total
		UK	Europe	World	
	L&W in the Gulf States & Saudi Arabia	£17.45	£19.45	£22.95	
	Living & Working in Ireland	£17.45	£19.45	£22.95	
	Living & Working in Italy	£17.45	£19.45	£22.95	
	Living and Working in London	£14.45	£16.45	£19.95	
	Living & Working in New Zealand	£17.45	£19.45	£22.95	
	Living & Working in Spain	£17.45	£19.45	£22.95	
	Living & Working in Switzerland	£17.45	£19.45	£22.95	
	Making a Living in France	£14.45	£16.45	£19.95	
	Making a Living in Spain	£14.45	£16.45	£19.95	
	Renovating Your French Home	£17.45	£19.45	£22.95	
	Retiring in France	£14.45	£16.45	£19.95	
	Retiring in Spain	£14.45	£16.45	£19.95	
	Rural Living in France	£14.45	£16.45	£19.95	
	Shooting Caterpillars in Spain	£10.45	£12.45	£15.95	
	Surprised by France	£12.45	£14.45	£17.95	
	Wild Thyme in Ibiza	£10.45	£12.45	£15.95	
				Total	

Order your copies today by phone, fax, post or email from: Survival Books, PO Box 3780, YEOVIL, BA21 5WX, United Kingdom. (☎▤ +44 (0)1935-700060, ⊠ sales@survivalbooks.net, ⌨ www.survivalbooks.net). If you aren't entirely satisfied, simply return them to us within 14 days for a full and unconditional refund.

I enclose a cheque in payment/Please charge my Amex/Delta/Maestro (Switch)/ MasterCard/Visa card as follows. (delete as applicable)

Card No. _ _ _ _   _ _ _ _   _ _ _ _ _ _ _ _ **Security Code***_ _ _

Expiry date ____ / ____ **Issue number(Maestro/Switch only)** _____

Signature _____ **Tel. No.** _____

NAME _____

ADDRESS _____

* The security code is the last three digits on the signature strip.